6-14   6⁰⁰

22

PAINTERS

EBERHARD ROTERS

OF THE BAUHAUS

PRAEGER PUBLISHERS

NEW YORK · WASHINGTON

BOOKS THAT MATTER

Translated from the German by Anna Rose Cooper

PUBLISHED IN THE UNITED STATES OF AMERICA IN 1969
BY PRAEGER PUBLISHERS, INC.
111 FOURTH AVENUE, NEW YORK, N. Y. 10003
SECOND PRINTING
© 1965 IN BERLIN, GERMANY, BY REMBRANDT VERLAG
ALL RIGHTS RESERVED
LIBRARY OF CONGRESS CATALOG CARD NUMBER : 69-15385
PRINTED IN GERMANY

TABLE OF CONTENTS

INTRODUCTION

'All the arts culminate in architecture', begins the Bauhaus manifesto of 1919, written by the architect Walter Gropius. Yet it is the painters of the Bauhaus—Klee, Kandinsky, Feininger, Itten, Moholy-Nagy, Albers—who attract most attention, are discussed in lectures, magazines, and books, and whose paintings are known throughout the world, while the architects are often ignored. Over the years, the concept *Bauhaus painter* has come to have a universally accepted meaning.

Gropius' manifesto continues:

> In the past, the ornamentation of buildings was considered to be the major function of the visual arts. They played a vital rôle in the creation of great architecture. Today, these arts stand in a self-sufficient isolation from which they can be redeemed only by conscious co-operation and mutual understanding between all those involved. Architects, painters and sculptors must rediscover and understand the many-sided aspects of building, both as a whole and in all its parts; only then will their work be informed with that architectonic spirit which was lost in salon art.

This assertion that a building must be a complete whole created by the harmonious co-operation of all the arts was a challenge not so much to architects as to painters and sculptors. These artists had in the past worked in close collaboration with architects and master builders from the very inception of a project. But they had been gradually displaced from the building process, and were now completely divorced from integration with the crafts.

The manifesto was inspired by the vision of a kind of guild devoted to the erection of a twentieth-century cathedral—a building which would be contemporary in appearance and function, a new type of organic structure created by the integration of all the arts and perfectly expressing the totality of the contemporary social situation.

Mies van der Rohe crystallized these thoughts in a speech on the occasion of Gropius' seventieth birthday on May 18, 1953, at the Blackstone Hotel in Chicago, when he said: 'The Bauhaus was not an institute with a clear programme, it was an idea. Gropius himself formulated this idea with great precision in these words: "Art and technology— a new unity."'

The front page of the Bauhaus manifesto was illustrated by a woodcut by Lyonel Feininger representing the 'Cathedral of Socialism': a church with spire, against a background of stars. In the expressionist disruption of its diagonals, it suggests *The Cabinet of Dr. Caligari* rather than the ordered rationality of architecture and technology.

The cathedral buildings of the Middle Ages—in Paris, Amiens and Reims, Bamberg and Naumburg, Pisa, Siena, and Florence—as well as the churches and palaces of the Baroque period, were created by the combined efforts of generations of artists. Their sculptural ornamentation, their stained glass and altars, were the means by which these architectural masterpieces achieved final perfection. Seeking a similar perfection, the builders of the pseudo-Gothic cathedrals of the late nineteenth century borrowed external detail from previous epochs—Greek capitals, Gothic triforia—fitting them together in various permutations, like pieces from a toy building-set. The inevitable outcome was pretentious buildings of a platitudinous banality, the product of a pedantic academic outlook limited to the rigid imitation of traditional styles.

This is why Gropius decided to abandon the sterile vocabulary of an artistic language which had lost its meaning. He did not want to imitate the building styles of past epochs, but to create the conditions necessary for the evolution of a new architectonic outlook. His idea of a 'cathedral', therefore, did not envisage derivative façade decoration, but a whole work with a life of its own, created by a corporate body of artists and craftsmen and manifestly the result of the interaction of their related activities. For this, he needed the painters. When the Bauhaus was founded in 1919, there were more painters than architects on its teaching staff. Besides Gropius himself, the architecture department had only one other teacher, Adolf Meyer.

There is a common bond between the painters who taught at the Bauhaus. This is most evident when one considers the notable painters of that period who did *not* belong to the Bauhaus, such as the Brücke artists, or Emil Nolde and Oskar Kokoschka. This kind of Expressionism—wild, ecstatic, sensational—had no representation in the Bauhaus. The choice made by Gropius betrays the architect. Most of the painters who taught at the Bauhaus came from southern and western Germany, or at least, like the foreigners—Wassily Kandinsky and Lyonel Feininger—received their artistic education there. This common background may help to explain a basic stylistic homogeneity. All the painters working at the Bauhaus, without exception, wrestled with the same creative problems as arise in architecture, and this 'elective affinity' with architecture is far from accidental. This is true both of Lyonel Feininger's transcendental dream buildings and of Oskar Schlemmer's space-dividing sets for his imaginary puppet theatre. Johannes Itten's system of art education is permeated by the spirit of analysis and organization, as are his paintings. The same can be said of the screenlike scaffoldings characteristic of many of Georg Muche's early compositions. In Paul Klee's drawings and water-colours, basic architectural principles, such as supports, loads, equilibrium, stress, mass and space, and repetition and contrast, are applied to create playful anecdotes, fairy-tales, and whimsical fantasies, while Wassily Kandinsky's paintings express these same principles as moods and symbols of human experience. In the Constructivist works of Laszlo Moholy-Nagy and Josef Albers, architectural laws are applied in the pictorial projection on a flat plane.

A book about the Bauhaus painters would have little point if it merely described episodes from the lives of artists whose careers ran for a short time along parallel lines. But the Bauhaus was not a railway junction for developing artists in transit. It was a focal meeting point where artistic destinies were shaped and given direction. Individual artists exerted a strong influence on the Bauhaus atmosphere by their personal aura. In some cases, their mere presence was sufficient; indeed, it was considered essential for its catalytic effect. This explains how the reluctant Feininger was persuaded to move from Weimar to Dessau, without any obligation to teach, for the sole purpose of making his influence felt by his presence. On the other hand, the individual artists were profoundly influenced by their colleagues, and all of them underwent a process of clarification and maturing of ideas, which enabled them to develop unrealized potentialities in their creative work. The mutual exchange of experiences among artists had a great deal to do with this, but there were two other important factors: teaching, and practical work in the Bauhaus workshops.

The painters had become college professors. They gave lectures. These painters, who had been used to discussing the background of their art with perhaps a few like-minded artists and connoisseurs, suddenly had to stand up in front of a class of students—some enthusiastic, others critical—and convey to them the essence and meaning of what was, at that time, still a very unfamiliar and revolutionary outlook. They had to start by establishing their artistic aims in their own minds, before they could translate these ideas into simple, precise, and easily understood language. The preparation of lectures thus forced the artists into an intellectual assessment of their own creative work. These experiences produced a new and up-to-date teaching system in art education. Its foundation was laid by Johannes Itten, a pupil of Adolf Hölzel. Itten—a pedagogical genius—organized the basic course, using methods which he based on his master's teachings. Both Paul Klee's *Pädagogisches Skizzenbuch* (Pedagogical Sketchbook) and Kandinsky's *Punkt und Linie zu Fläche* (Point and Line to Plane), which owe their origin to Bauhaus lectures, have become textbooks for the student of twentieth-century art.

While teaching gave the painters a theoretical basis for their artistic philosophy, their practical work in the Bauhaus workshops gave them the chance to experiment and to test their creative ideas. Problems with which they had grappled as painters on the two-dimensional plane could now be explored in other media. Oskar Schlemmer expressed his preoccupation with the changing relationship between the human form and its surroundings not only in his paintings—the apparent choreography of his painted figures was translated into real movement by flesh-and-blood dancers. So a dream was fulfilled, and Schlemmer's experiments led to the memorable developments of the Bauhaus stage. The Constructivist Laszlo Moholy-Nagy was led in a different direction by his studies in the field of communications theory. He designed a new typography, and he explored possibilities of artistic expression in photography and film and the effectiveness of advertising in these media.

The Bauhaus was an idea. Over the years, the idea has grown into a legend. While the present generation can understand this idea, it is not so easy for them to appreciate the richly orchestrated symphony that was the Bauhaus, with all its polyphony and overtones. A reconstruction from this distance in time may fill the gap and provide an opportunity for a relaxed and objective evaluation, although there is the danger of oversimplification. As an idea, the Bauhaus meant essentially the same thing for most of the participants, but as an experience, its impact was obviously totally different on each individual. From our present vantage-point, we see before us a panorama of intersecting perspectives, resulting from the meeting of many artistic personalities with differing backgrounds and styles. Such an atmosphere favoured a constant cross-fertilization of ideas, and each artist in turn influenced the others and was influenced by them. The fact that the Bauhaus painters felt impelled to concern themselves with matters quite remote from painting bears out the logic of the apparently absurd decision to appoint painters to the staff of a college primarily founded for the teaching of architecture. However, in the last resort, it was the only solution, as there were practically no young architects at that time who could have understood and taught Gropius' ideas. He was right in expecting to find this understanding among the leading painters of Expressionism and Constructivism. His trust was not misplaced. Their imagination and creative intelligence gave them an insight into the laws which govern artistic endeavour in every field.

WALTER GROPIUS AND THE BAUHAUS

To fathom the extent of the Bauhaus painters' influence on the contemporary scene, we must begin by examining the institute and its founder. Walter Gropius is an exceptional personality, who brought to life a unique vision by taking advantage of the particular artistic situation of a memorable period of history.

The Period The *Staatliches Bauhaus Weimar* (State School of Building, Weimar) was founded in 1919. On March 20 of that year, the Art Academy of the Grand Duchy of Saxony changed its name to *Staatliches Bauhaus Weimar*, and a month later, Walter Gropius was appointed Director. In the same year, he published its syllabus, the 'Program of the State Bauhaus of Weimar'.

The first year of peace after World War I—1919—was a year of reflection and stocktaking in Germany, before the ferment of the 'roaring twenties'. Following on the revolution of November, 1918, it was the year of the Weimar Constitution and the democratic parliament which appointed Friedrich Ebert as first President of the Reich. The mood of the times may be gauged from the absurd pamphleteering activities of the Dadaist Johannes Baader, who went so far as to interrupt a parliamentary session. German Expressionism had reached the climax of its artistic revolution just before the war, with the First German Autumn Salon of 1913 in Herwarth Walden's Berlin *Sturm-Galerie* (Sturm Gallery). The horrors of the epoch had been foreshadowed by mystical visions, such as Ludwig Meidner's apocalyptic paintings, poems by Jacob van Hoddis, and Georg Heym's prophetic *Auferstanden ist er aus Gewölben tief* (From Deep Vaults He Is Arisen). The original upsurge of Expressionism had been stifled by the war. The year 1919 brought a spirit of re-appraisal and adjustment to a new order. It saw the publication of Richard Dehmel's war diary, *Zwischen Volk und Menschheit* (Between Nation and Mankind), Karl Kraus's satirical mammoth drama *Die letzten Tage der Menschheit* (The Last Days of Mankind), and Franz Werfel's play *Der Gerichtstag* (Judgement Day). Rudolf Steiner the anthroposophist tried to give society a new sense of purpose in his *Die Kernpunkte der sozialen Frage* (The Core of the Social Problem). Paul Fechter, a well-known critic, reviewed the new movement in his essay *Der Expressionismus*, which was the first critical assessment of Expressionism, although Hermann Bahr had attempted a poetic interpretation in 1912. But now the 'November Group' had been founded in Berlin as a rallying point for the generation of young artists returned from the war. This became the prototype of similar groups which were springing up throughout provincial Germany. The artistic scene was dominated by social criticism (George Grosz, Otto Dix), and radical and semi-anarchist tendencies (Kurt Schwitters, Raoul Hausmann, and the Dada group). Though constructive elements were gaining ground in painting and sculpture, Constructivism itself did not make a final breakthrough until 1922–23, when a number of artists emigrated to Berlin from Russia as a consequence of official Soviet cultural policy.

The Youth Movement, which had begun with the *Wandervogel* and had made rapid strides in popularity since the turn of the century, had reached its peak in 1913 with the youth festival on the Hohe Meissner. After 1919, its various internal factions became more and more differentiated, resulting in the break-up of the movement into a number of separate organizations. Small groups of disciples collected around itinerant preachers and eccentric holy men, such as 'world reformers' Louis Haeusser and Leonard Starck who, with their flowing manes and unconventional dress, brought ridicule on themselves and their avowed aim of reviving the socialism of the early Christians. All of these elements were woven into the backdrop of the period in which the Bauhaus was founded.

The Artistic Situation   Art history can be seen to follow its own dialectic process of development. The foundation of the Bauhaus was the climax of a reaction against the historicism which had dominated art in the second half of the nineteenth century. Contemporary scholarship has not yet fully evaluated the unique quality of the nineteenth century, when an era of democratic national rebirth followed the Napoleonic Wars, and Romanticism in the arts mirrored the proud achievements of the bourgeoisie inspired by the French Revolution. By the 1860's, this had finally degenerated into the banal Biedermeier style fashionable among the petit bourgeoisie during the restoration. An extravagant and eccentric national pride, with its roots in the past, flourished side by side with a scientific outlook which found its philosophic expression in positivism and empiricism. This led to popular acceptance of a somewhat shallow philosophy couched in the jargon of the natural sciences, which encouraged the man in the street to take pride in the material progress of the machine age—an age which started not only with noise, smoke, and a naïve optimism, but also with dusty furniture in overstuffed parlours furnished in styles varying from 'Olde German' to Renaissance or Baroque. Since the period of Chippendale, there had been a decline in original inspiration in architecture, in the crafts, and in the decorative arts. Creative freedom had been threatened and restricted by the all-pervasive vogue of imitation; but at last there were signs of rebellion against this artistic strait-jacket. The revolt started in England. Around the middle of the nineteenth century, John Ruskin advocated a return to genuine craftsmanship and to simple forms. With William Morris, Ruskin published designs for use by architects and craftsmen. William Crane, a friend of Morris, also contributed to the revival of design in craftsmanship. This was the start of a movement which made rapid strides in its struggle against the degeneration of European art, and which originated a style of dynamically mobile ornamentation inspired by simple organic forms. From these beginnings, just before the turn of the century, came the *Jugendstil* or *art nouveau* movement. Within a decade, it had exerted tremendous influence in all spheres of the arts, including applied art in the widest sense—notably, interior decoration, ceramics, and book design. An astonished public called it the 'Secession style'; years later, this term was used in Germany to describe the newly built Kurfürstendamm in West Berlin.

The great names of the *Jugendstil* and *art nouveau* are, therefore, to be found among architects, interior designers, craftsmen, and book designers: Bruno Paul, Peter Behrens, Otto Eckmann, August Endell, Joseph Olbrich, and Richard Riemerschmidt, but above all, the great Henri van de Velde, born in Antwerp in 1863, whose writings distilled the essence of *art nouveau* philosophy, and whose designs expressed this style in its most developed form. The style's main strongholds were Glasgow, Paris, Vienna, Munich, Berlin, Darmstadt, and, last but not least, Weimar. It was characterized by two opposing features: on the one hand, overlavish ornamentation based on luxuriantly curving plant forms, which tended to conceal the basic structure; on the other hand, emphasis of an object's function by the use of clear and simple forms with little ornamentation. The latter trend finally prevailed, paving the way for *Gebrauchskunst* (utilitarian art), and this in turn was echoed later in painting and sculpture by the Constructivist style.

The revival of functional art was heralded by the foundation of a number of new craft workshops. The United Workshops for Arts and Crafts were set up in Munich in 1897; in 1898, Karl Schmid started the Dresden Workshops for Arts and Crafts; these were followed in 1906 by the Hellerau Workshops near Dresden. In 1903, the Vienna Secession resulted in the establishment of the *Wiener Werkstätte* (Vienna Workshop) under the management of Joseph Hoffmann and Coloman Moser, who expressly based their philosophy on pre-Morris and pre-Ruskin ideas. In 1907, twelve artists and twelve manufacturers formed the German Werkbund, which still exists today. It was the last and most important foundation of this type before the advent of the Bauhaus. According to its statutes, the aim of the Werkbund was 'to raise the standard of manufactured products by the joint efforts of art, industry and craftsmanship, by means of education, propaganda, and a united stand on all questions of mutual interest'. Here we have the seeds of the ideas which later flowered in the Bauhaus. They were summarized by Friedrich Naumann in *Deutsche Gewerbekunst* (German Applied Arts, Berlin, 1908) in the following words:

> Better to lay construction bare than to hide it. From now on, a spirit of fine and brutal honesty will prevail, to put an end to a lying epoch, which built with iron but simulated stone. A house shall be built from the inside outwards, a chair is to be made for sitting on. A room will be thought of as a whole, the cupboards shall not stand against the walls as foreign bodies, the table will be kinsman to the cupboard, the window will be part of the wall, and the stove will no longer be an ugly monster, while all the upholstery materials will blend with the woods used. What matters is not an academic unity of style, but the achievement of harmony.

For Gropius, the Bauhaus was an instrument for the realization of the utopian programs of 1907 and 1908.

The Man Walter Gropius was born in Berlin on May 18, 1883. His genius was nurtured in the soil of a family tradition which included craftsmen, clergymen, and schoolmasters among his forebears. His grandfather, Carl Wilhelm Gropius, was an architect and owner of a building firm, with a passion for painting, whose overriding criterion in all his work was the creation of an artistic whole. He was a close friend of Karl Friedrich Schinkel, who built the Old Museum in Berlin. In 1827, inspired by an invention by the photographer Louis Daguerre which he had seen in Paris, he built a Diorama in Berlin— a dramatic landscape screen, onto which were projected artistic lighting effects. A great-uncle, Martin Gropius, built the Berlin Museum of Arts and Crafts, and he was appointed Director of the Berlin School of Arts and Crafts in 1867. He consistently advocated good design in craftsmanship and, in the 1870's, published collections of decorative patterns for craftsmen. Walter Gropius' father was also an architect and a senior official in the State Building Department.

Gropius' childhood impressions were moulded in a period of radical changes in all the arts and crafts, and these early experiences helped to determine his future artistic course.

Meanwhile, the American scene had been transformed by the appearance of huge but well-proportioned industrial buildings which owed their majestic effect to their unadorned simplicity, and which derived a certain stark beauty from their functional design. The young Gropius, who was one of the first to recognize their importance, wrote many letters to Canada and the United States to obtain material for his studies. He summed up the results of his investigations in 1913, in an article entitled *Die Entwicklung der modernen Industriebaukunst* (The Development of Modern Industrial Architecture). His views on the *Gesamtkunstwerk* (integral work of art) as the joint product of the architect and the craftsman had now crystallized into ideas that were far in advance of the movements of artistic reform in Germany, France, and Britain, which were still overshadowed by the moribund *Jugendstil* or *art nouveau*. The period of constructive and functional form had begun.

Gropius studied architecture at the Institute of Technology in Berlin-Charlottenburg from 1903 to 1907. From then until 1910, he was in charge of Peter Behrens' architectural practice in Berlin. Behrens, who was born in Hamburg, was one of the few important German architects and designers produced by the generation before Gropius. In 1907, Behrens had been appointed general artistic adviser to the German General Electricity Company (AEG). His design of the AEG turbine and assembly sheds was revolutionary in outlook and signalled the birth of functional architecture in Germany. In Behrens' employment, Gropius acquired the basic practical experience for his own work. In 1910, he started his own architectural practice in Berlin, and his first big order came from the industrialist Karl Benscheid, who commissioned him to build the *Fagus-werke,* a shoe-last factory near Alfeld on the Leine. In this building, the twenty-eight-year-old architect made his first mature and complete stylistic statement; it represents a major advance on Behrens' buildings, which are ponderous and massive in comparison. In Gropius' building, the weight of the walls appears to be cancelled out, and the skeleton of the supporting metal construction is plainly revealed. In its combination of glass, metal, and brickwork, the whole building seems to be open to a constantly flowing interrelation between internal and external space, and it already contains the germ of the architectural conception of the Dessau Bauhaus.

In 1910, Gropius submitted to Walter Rathenau a program for a public housing project with a consistent artistic orientation. In his memorandum, he explained in broad outline his ideas for raising the standard of design in industrial production through the co-operation of artists and craftsmen.

In 1915, Henri van de Velde, the founding director of the School of Arts and Crafts of the Grand Duchy of Weimar, recommended Walter Gropius as his successor. Van de Velde wanted to leave Germany because of the increasing hostility he had encountered as a foreigner during the war. However, for the time being, the school was being used as a reserve field hospital. In January, 1916, at the invitation of the Ministry of the Grand Duchy of Saxony, Gropius submitted a typescript, *Proposals for the Foundation of a Teaching Institute as an Advisory Centre for Industry, Crafts and Trades.* It opened with a sweeping condemnation of the standard of craftsmanship as a result of industrial mass production, and it demanded:

> ... active co-operation between the artist, the businessman and the engineer which, if it were organized by modern methods, might eventually achieve the same function as that formerly fulfilled by individual workmanship. ... Until there is widespread recognition of these principles, the majority of industrialists will, unfortunately, continue to treat private artists with suspicion. On the other hand, it is not unreasonable to suppose that they would have more confidence in a teaching institute sponsored by the State as an artistic advisory centre under the direction of a well-known artist with technical experience.

This was followed by a precise exposition of the structure of such a school which, in fact, was identical with the program and curriculum of the Bauhaus (Wingler, *Das Bauhaus*, pp. 29 ff.).

The Bauhaus During the Bauhaus period, Weimar had about 30,000 inhabitants. Until the end of the war, it had been the official residence of the Grand Dukes of Saxony-Weimar-Eisenach. As in many other capitals of the small German states, the cultural atmosphere in Weimar was one of aristocratic refinement. Goethe's spiritual heritage continued to dominate the city's cultural life, and its influence seemed to grow year by year. The atmosphere was liberal,

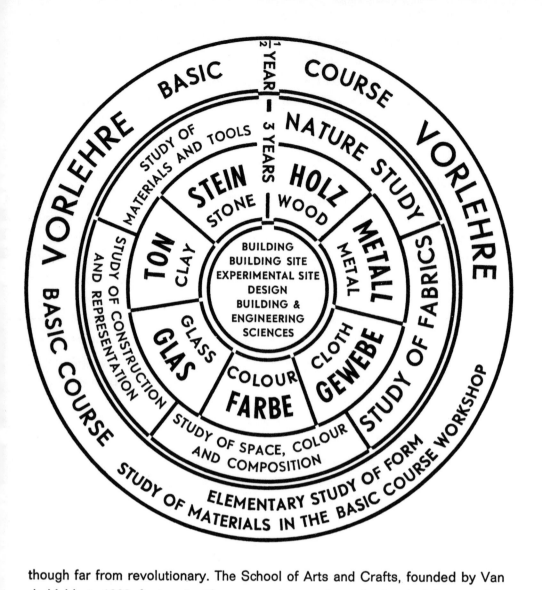

though far from revolutionary. The School of Arts and Crafts, founded by Van de Velde in 1906, first met with some resistance from the local philistines, but this was overcome as a result of the discreet blessing and encouragement which the Duke himself bestowed on the modern, progressive trend. The worthy professors Klemm, Engelhard, Hagen, and Mackensen expected Gropius to continue the respectable tradition established by Van de Velde. Instead, the new head conducted the school along such revolutionary lines that they were frequently mistaken as being communistic. It was, of course, inevitable that the Bauhaus would be subjected to critical scrutiny from every angle. But Gropius' ideas were really quite simple and logical: fresh inspiration for architecture, drawn from the dual forces of craftsmanship and art, the one precise and functional, the other creative and imaginative. Thus, architecture—the man-made part of man's environment—would, at last, mirror in true proportion the harmonious relationship between man and his works.

The organic structure of the curriculum is shown in the following schematic illustration devised by Gropius:

However, outsiders were startled and shocked by the completely new teaching method of free expression, which aimed at awakening and releasing the students' dormant creative powers by an unconventional individual approach and bold symbolism in the means of expression.

The history of the Bauhaus falls into four distinct periods: the Weimar Bauhaus; the Dessau Bauhaus under Gropius; the Dessau Bauhaus under Meyer; and the Dessau and Berlin Bauhaus under Mies van der Rohe.

1919	1920	1921	1922	1923	1924	1925	1926	1927	1928	1929	1930	1931	1932	1933
Weimar						Dessau								Berlin
			Gropius						Meyer		Mies v. d. Rohe			
Feininger														
Itten														
Marcks														
	Muche													
		Schlemmer												
			Klee											
			Schreyer											
				Kandinsky										
				Moholy-Nagy										
						Bayer								
						Albers								

The first period was dominated by Expressionism, the second by Constructivism, the third by Functionalism, and the fourth by architecture.

The Weimar period (1919–24) was the happiest and most exciting. Despite financial difficulties, it stands out as a glowing and boisterous time, illuminated by the first flush of enthusiasm of a new beginning. The experiments made in that period eventually formed the basis for the teaching program, which gradually evolved into a firmer pattern. A fervent splendour characterized the Weimar period. The highly talented though heterogeneous student body consisted of a colourful assortment of boy scouts, ramblers, food cranks, world reformers, and idealists of all shades of ideological persuasion. There was a constant ferment of passionate though friendly argument. Most of the painters attached to the Bauhaus came from the direction of mature Expressionism: Lyonel Feininger, Johannes Itten, Georg Muche, Oskar Schlemmer, Paul Klee, Lothar Schreyer, Wassily Kandinsky, and Laszlo Moholy-Nagy.

Siegfried Giedion described this period in his biography of Walter Gropius in the following words:

> The fate of the Bauhaus is involved in a tragic contradiction. Nowhere else would the director of a state organization have been permitted the

freedom, given to Walter Gropius from the outset, to carry through such an uncompromising project and to call in the best talents from wherever they might be. On the other hand, probably nowhere else would this have given rise to such violent opposition.

The solid citizens of Weimar, who had supported the Nazis from an early stage, saw to it that the Weimar Bauhaus was dissolved. The 1924 elections brought to power in Thuringia a right-wing coalition of nationalist parties. Their cultural policies encouraged the type of sentimental, popular-nationalist kitsch which followed Ludwig Thoma and Karl Haider. This school of thought was well supported in Thuringia, with its background of small family firms engaged in manufacture and handicrafts. It was enthusiastically endorsed by every frustrated painter with a chip on his shoulder. Paul Schultze-Naumburg, for instance, became one of its most militant exponents. At the end of 1924, the Weimar Bauhaus was forced to close by the Thuringian Provincial Assembly; on reading through the minutes of the proceedings and the testimonies, one cannot help feeling that this was the revenge of the small cabinet-makers.

'Art and technology—a new unity.' This was the motto of the Bauhaus Exhibition of 1923, and it could equally well be used to describe the next period in the history of the Bauhaus: the years 1925–28 at Dessau under Gropius. Here, the Bauhaus expanded and consolidated its internal structure. A down-to-earth atmosphere of self-confidence, sobriety, and purposefulness replaced the hectic fervour, overwrought ideology, and religiosity that had left their mark on the intensive work of the first few years. The Bauhaus became a laboratory for the development of industrial design and of prototypes for mass production, and great care was taken to strike a happy balance between the aesthetic and the functional. Naturally, there were no hard-and-fast rules, and the process was quite elastic, since freedom to experiment within the context of artistic expression was the overriding consideration. In 1926, the Bauhaus, which had been classed as an institute, was granted university status. The teachers gave up their title of 'master', with its medieval associations with craft guilds and masonic lodges, and were appointed professors. Teachers and students had grown closer to each other, and, for the first time, former students joined the teaching staff.

Dessau, in the province of Anhalt, was rather different in character from Weimar. Although its town centre and ducal residence bore the imprint of Weinbrenner's classicism, in the same way as Weimar did, and its cultural tradition also went back to the period of the Enlightenment, Dessau, unlike rural Weimar, lay within a well-developed industrial belt stretching from Leipzig, Halle, and Magdeburg to Berlin. The town itself had expanded into an industrial centre in its own right, with approximately 70,000 inhabitants. It had the Junckers works, with Agfa-Wolffen nearby.

On May 25, 1925, the town council of Dessau decided to take over the Bauhaus. This was made possible only by the initiative and tireless activity of the mayor, Fritz Hesse, who had been made aware of the significance of the Bauhaus by Ludwig Grote, the art historian. The first idea of amalgamating it with the Dessau School of Arts and Crafts was soon abandoned, and, at last, the Bauhaus was able to put up its own buildings with funds provided by the town council. Gropius drew up the plans in 1925; by March, 1926, the major building work was completed, and the school was in residence by October. The solemn ceremony of inauguration took place on December 4, 1926. This masterpiece of Gropius—the teaching block and staff houses—gave visible expression to the constructive spirit of the Dessau Bauhaus. The teaching block, whose interior, as it were, enclosed its outer space in a threefold movement, was architecturally the pure expression of collaborative work. While each section of the building was individually emphasized, all three stood in dynamic harmony with the others, forming a triangular pattern around a central axis.

The painters who remained at the Dessau Bauhaus continued to exert a decisive influence on the shaping of policy, but one particular stylistic tendency —Constructivism—had become dominant. Itten and Schreyer had left the Bauhaus while it was still at Weimar. Muche followed in 1927. Internal disagreements were responsible for the departure of these three artistic personalities from the Bauhaus. Had they stayed, they might have altered its course. Although we may regret that they did not do so, their ideas were almost certainly out of tune with contemporary trends. Feininger had been persuaded to move to Dessau, but without any teaching commitments, and although he played no active part in it, the life of the Bauhaus was enriched by his quiet presence. He could almost be called the guardian angel of the Bauhaus. The painters now active on the teaching staff all showed Constructivist tendencies during this period. This is true of Klee's work, as well as of Kandinsky's and of Schlemmer's but can be seen most clearly in Moholy-Nagy's output and in the experiments of ex-students Josef Albers and Herbert Bayer, who had recently joined the staff.

On February 4, 1928, to the consternation of the students, Gropius announced his resignation. He was weary from the long struggle for the Bauhaus and all the red tape that it had involved. He also believed that the Bauhaus idea had become sufficiently established to ensure its survival without his guidance. The man Gropius intended as his successor was the Swiss architect Hannes Meyer, who had been teaching at the Bauhaus since 1927, and who took over the leadership on April 1, 1928.

Experience has shown that, with few exceptions (such as Gropius and Le Corbusier), the majority of modern architects lack an appreciation of painting. With its emphasis on strictly functional design, twentieth-century architecture has given the aesthetic outlook of architects an utilitarian bias. They will accept paintings, not for their intrinsic value, but as ornaments on a wall, an added interior decoration. This explains why so many architects are highly successful at designing their own living space down to the smallest detail, including the picture frames—but not the pictures within these frames. Being primarily intended as a coloured spot on the wall, the painting itself is usually meaningless. This mentality seems to have determined Hannes Meyer's attitude to painting: not hostile but indifferent, and without any comprehension of Gropius' original vision of the creative integration of the arts. Under Meyer's direction, the Bauhaus increasingly assumed the character of a college of technology for architecture and the building trades, with purist overtones. Its work became influenced more by sociological considerations, with special emphasis on urban planning. Not surprisingly, only three painters—Klee, Kandinsky, and Albers—outlasted the Meyer period (1928–30), apart from Feininger, who had, of course, given up teaching.

Meyer had many enemies. As Director of the Bauhaus, he ran into trouble trying to run the school in accordance with his own Spartan leanings, though it was generally agreed that he was an honest and upright man. He was a Marxist and believed in scientific materialism. He expressed himself clearly and logically, but in an aggressive manner. His imagination tended to run along narrow practical lines, and he rejected as formalistic most of the ideals inherited from the Gropius period. In May, 1930, for tactical reasons, he dissolved the student Communist group. He was not a member of any party, but he never made a secret of his political opinions, and was unable to reconcile the stresses caused by party political antagonisms among the students. The town council of Dessau, not without justification, was afraid of a crisis developing, and dismissed Meyer from his post on April 1, 1930.

On Gropius' recommendation, Mies van der Rohe was appointed as Meyer's successor. The famous architect, born in Aachen in 1886, who was living in Berlin at the time, became head of the Bauhaus on April 5, 1930. Under his direction (1930–33), formal discipline was tightened up, but he, too, was unable to suppress the fierce political tension between the extremes of right and left which pervaded every aspect of life at the time. The nationalists, who had become dominant in the Dessau parliament, succeeded in forcing the closure of the Bauhaus in 1932, although Hesse, the mayor, vainly attempted to save it. The contracts were cancelled with effect from October 1. Mies van der Rohe continued to run the Bauhaus as a private establishment, reopening it in the Berlin suburb of Steglitz in a former telephone factory. Teaching was resumed there in the autumn of 1932, but on April 11, 1933, the Nazis searched the building on a writ from the Dessau State Prosecutor and ordered its provisional closure. On July 29, 1933, Mies van der Rohe issued a statement announcing that he was compelled 'to dissolve the Berlin Bauhaus as a result of economic difficulties caused by the suspension of its activities'.

The last painters to teach at the Bauhaus were Wassily Kandinsky and Josef Albers, Paul Klee having left in 1931 to take up an appointment at the Düsseldorf Academy.

LYONEL FEININGER

Lyonel Feininger was the first of the Bauhaus masters. He arrived in Weimar in May, 1919. He had been Gropius' first choice, no doubt because there was a close spiritual affinity between the two men, and Gropius saw in the painter's work a medium for his own ideas. The lucidity with which Feininger was able to illustrate transcendental buildings was in tune with Gropius' conception of the harmonious clarity which should govern the architecture of the future house of man.

In Weimar and beyond, polite society was shocked. Even the officials who had initially approved Gropius' plan now had second thoughts. They could sense a spirit of rebellion in Feininger's art which refused to run along the narrow tracks of cautious middle-class 'good sense'. Wilhelm von Bode, Director-General of Museum in Berlin, who had been instrumental in introducing a number of reforms into art colleges after the war, had given Gropius a good reference, but now he wrote indignantly to the former Lord Marshal, Baron von Fritsch, who passed on the complaint to the Weimar authorities:

> The goings-on at the Bauhaus about which I have been reading in the newspapers, must have given your Excellency a peculiar impression as to my own views on art and my reliability as a referee. I am horrified! When Gropius made his first appointment—of Feininger, the Cubist—I lost no time in telling him how astonished I was. Gropius had submitted a program to me which, though tending to be somewhat radical, I thought was acceptable on the whole. He enlarged on it verbally, saying that, like me, he was mainly interested in the revival of craftsmanship, and, for a start, he would appoint only competent craftsmen to give the young people a thorough grounding in their trades. Fine art would have to wait its turn! And now, the first thing he does is to appoint Feininger (Wingler, *Das Bauhaus*, p. 42).

Feininger was labelled a Cubist—a most damning indictment!

Those who saw in him a revolutionary were quite right, but paradoxically, his revolutionary spirit was expressed in terms of the utmost caution and restraint. With his long, gentle face, this German-American radiated a quiet goodness. He was so shy that he would never attend the opening day of exhibitions of his own works but would go later, incognito. He blushed to have his inmost feelings displayed in public. His personal reserve is reflected graphologically in his handwriting, which gives the impression of a delicate trellis. In his letters, one finds frequent full stops (a sign of cautious delimitation) and dashes (indicating reflectiveness). His writing recalls the open texture of his paintings.

Feininger loved Weimar. Having previously lived there for a short time, he felt completely at home in the town and its surrounding villages, where he found the peace that his quiet nature craved. In 1905, he started to visit Julia Berg, a student at Van de Velde's art college in Weimar. She became Feininger's second wife in 1908. For some time after that, he continued to travel to and fro between Berlin and Weimar. It was in Weimar in 1913 that he perfected his distinctive style: *Gelmeroda I* (Hess, No. 98 in the catalogue), which he painted after numerous sketches of the church in the nearby hamlet of that name, represents a turning-point in his development.

Lyonel Feininger was forty-eight when he joined the Bauhaus. He was born in New York on July 17, 1871. His father, Charles Feininger—the son of a German immigrant from Baden—was a well-known violinist, and his mother, Elisabeth Cecilia Lutz, a famous singer. Their son inherited from them his feeling for music, which exerted a strong influence on his work as a painter. It cannot be mere coincidence that the same is true of other Expressionist painters, for example, Paul Klee. In 1887, Feininger went to Europe, where his parents were engaged on a lengthy concert tour. He remained in Germany until 1936. In 1888, after a short period at the Hamburg School of Arts and Crafts, he became a student at the Berlin Academy. Berlin was to remain his home for many years. In 1889, his first drawings appeared in the *Humoristische Blätter*. For several years, he seemed to be destined for the career of a successful cartoonist. Grotesque and satirical drawings on topical subjects were published in Berlin comic papers such as *Ulk* and *Lustige Blätter,* and these were taken up by American publications. He left the Berlin Academy in 1891, and went to Paris the following year. In 1905, he first met Julia Berg, and returned to Paris with her in 1906. He became a habitué of the Café du Dôme, which was the meeting-place of the German artists' colony in Paris. He painted his first picture in 1907—a china monkey. His artistic career now entered an entirely new phase; he gave up caricature and took up painting. In 1908, while on a visit to London (where he married Julia), he was greatly impressed by Turner's paintings. Meanwhile, he continued to make frequent journeys to Weimar, which had first attracted him about 1906. On one of these journeys, in 1913, he went on the first of his many study trips around the tiny villages in the vicinity of Weimar, some of which are too small to be shown on the map: Gelmeroda, Hopfgarten, Tröbsdorf, Mellingen, Markvippach, Vollersroda, Possendorf, Klein-Kromsdorf, Niedergrundstedt, Legefeld, Umpferstedt, Eichelborn, Tiefurt, Gaberndorf, Kiliansroda, Öttern, Denstedt, and Zottelstedt. This was a momentous year for him, when he discovered his own individual style. He now came to the notice of the Blaue Reiter artists, and Franz Marc invited him to show his paintings with this group in Herwarth Walden's First German Autumn Salon at the Sturm Gallery in Berlin. Feininger continued to keep in touch with the Blaue Reiter group and the Sturm circle; these were his points of contact with the European artistic revolution of his generation. In 1914, while he was considering moving to Weimar with his family, war broke out. Feininger stayed in Berlin. As an American, he was a member of a foreign nation—neutral for the time being. One must pay tribute to Herwarth Walden's courage in organizing Feininger exhibitions in 1916 and 1917, right in the middle of the war. Feininger joined the 'November

Group' in 1918. He met Gropius, and, at last, fate was kind to him. His dearest wish was granted—the chance to move to Weimar.

Feininger's art had matured. Three themes were dominant: landscape—including marine subjects with boats and ships—architecture, and the human form. The latter was, however, of least importance in his work, which includes only a small proportion of portraits and paintings where the human form predominates; these were mostly done in his early period. The key pictures are the *Kopf in Architektur* (Head in Architecture, Hess, No. 169), of 1917, and the moving *Bildnis eines tragischen Wesens* (Portrait of a Tragic Being, Hess, No. 212), of 1920. In both instances, the individual's free will seems to be negated by its subordination to the determinism of an all-powerful structure. Elsewhere, Feininger's people are either puppets or tiny observers almost lost in their surroundings. Feininger was a lonely puppet-master who experienced people not as individuals but as types and grotesque masks, and he watched them with ironic melancholy from a distance. His drawings confirm this view of himself; in *The Chicago Sunday Tribune*, he caricatured himself as a puppeteer manipulating the creatures of his invention. His earliest work may be likened to a miniature stage with constantly shifting scenes, peopled by loose-jointed, puppet-like figures on invisible strings, wearing stylized accessories: top hats, sombreros, conical capes. They included symbolic types, such as the pair of contrasting figures—one tall and thin (the artist), the other short and fat (his foil), and a medley of diplomats, cyclists, sportscar drivers, and little men drawn against a background of small and bizarre locomotives. The same tragi-comic figures, with that strangely lost air, later made a come-back as inhabitants of the toy towns which the artist carved for his son Andreas during the Bauhaus period. In some of Feininger's pictures, even the human beings seem like marionettes, their jerky movements frozen in a moment of time. This can be seen in *Kanalisationsloch* (Manhole, Hess, No. 31), of 1908, and in later paintings such as *Radfahrern* (Bicycle Race, Hess, No. 94), of 1912, and *Dame in Mauve* (Lady in Mauve, Hess, No. 227), dated 1922—where a mannequin display, cut out of glass and transparent paper, seems to glide as if on rails from right to left—and in *Kleine Maske* (Small Mask, Hess, No. 269), of 1926, in which the figure looms out of its dark background. In his early cartoons, there are echoes of the contemporary idiom of the *Jugendstil* or *art nouveau*, and while Feininger's personal style is unmistakable, one is reminded of the quality of line and representational standard of the work of Bruno Paul, Thomas Theodor Heine, and other contemporary draughtsmen.

His first attempt at pure architectural painting, in 1907, was abandoned. Then followed the period between 1908 and 1913, when hyperbolical type-figures, deriving from the distortions of caricature, dominated his style which, however, began to show an increasingly tighter crystallization of form. In 1912, he painted the first pictures which foreshadow his future artistic development in all its individuality—architectural pictures such as *Teltow I* (Hess, No. 86) and *Benz*

(Hess, No. 90), and coastline motifs with boats, such as *Am Quai* (On the Quai, Hess, No. 32), and *Landesteg* (Pier, Hess, No. 96). The turning-point, when he finally committed himself to a consistent style in his art, was 1913. In this year, he painted *Gelmeroda I, II,* and *III* (Hess, Nos. 98, 101, 102), and the strangely mysterious *Badende I* (Bathers I, Hess, No. 109), which anticipates his later conception of form.

From this point onward, his work continued to grow in refinement and depth. By the time he joined the Bauhaus, Feininger had behind him a sizable output. Two styles of composition are clearly discernible: the one brittle, restless; the other maintaining a quiet tension. They alternate throughout his life's work. The restless style is characterized by numerous broken diagonals and stippled, vibrating, somewhat clouded colour effects. Good examples of this style— which predominated before 1919–20—are *Umpferstedt I* and *II* (Hess, Nos. 119, 120). With growing maturity, his style developed a feeling of calm strength and controlled tension, produced by analytical breakdown into planes of generous proportions. This style became more prominent during the Bauhaus period.

But it was not as a painter that Feininger taught at the Bauhaus. He was 'master of form' in charge of the graphic workshop, with the technical master, Carl Zaubitzer. Feininger had started etching in 1905, while his first woodcuts date from 1918. Their number grew rapidly after the war. His friendship with Erich Heckel and Karl Schmidt-Rottluff may possibly have provided the impetus toward this art form. In this medium, too, his favourite motifs were buildings and sailing boats. He liked to print small woodcuts, which he used as vignettes for his letterheads. On his arrival in Weimar in the spring of 1919, he wrote enthusiastically to Julia: 'But do you know what is most wonderful here? The new workshop! Gropius is so kind! He let me have it straightaway. He showed me round the whole school, and I saw the etching workshop too. Oh, isn't it marvellous! You know, we shall be living in a painter's paradise here!' (Hess, *Lyonel Feininger*, p. 88).

In another letter to Julia, dated July 14, 1919, he writes about his responsibilities toward the students:

> In half an hour's time, a young man is coming to see me who wants to become my pupil—I told you about him yesterday. He looked at me as if I was his saviour. But what can even the best art teacher give except direction, support and development for a talent which is already there? Only rarely can one speak of God's gift; most of the time it is nothing but a struggle for years, decades, if a real artist is to emerge, and not just a clever artisan. What I would like best of all would be a stubborn pupil who has the strength of character to be himself. If he is any good, he will learn obedience from necessity, rather than from me; I do not want to mould docile disciples. (Wingler, *Das Bauhaus*, p. 43.)

Single-handed, Feininger organized an exhibition of students' graphic work, and he describes the preparations in his letter to Julia of June 27, 1919:

At last, I finished setting up the graphic exhibition yesterday afternoon, and it has turned out quite presentable after all. For three days, from eight in the morning till nine at night, I was standing there, removing from their large frames the etchings and photographs of great masters' works which normally adorn the Bauhaus corridors. I had to cut sheets of paper to the right size for mounts, and then I sorted and stuck on several hundred notices, drawings, watercolours and woodcuts. Finally, without help from anyone, I put them all back in the frames and nailed them up. (Wingler, *Das Bauhaus*, p. 43.)

The most permanent memorial we have of the Bauhaus printshop under Feininger is a series of graphic portfolios. The first of these was published in 1921 and contained twelve woodcuts by Feininger. In 1922, Kandinsky had his *Kleine Welten* (Small Worlds) printed in the Bauhaus workshop for the *Propyläen-Verlag* (Propyläen Press). In 1923, the newly founded *Bauhaus-Verlag* (Bauhaus Press) published woodcuts as illustrations to Simrock's *Wielandlied*. These were the work of the sculptor Gerhard Marcks, who was in charge of the Bauhaus pottery at Dornburg. Between 1921 and 1923, the Bauhaus Press published a series of portfolios under the title *Neue europäische Graphik* (New European Graphics), now generally known as the Bauhaus portfolios, which have become collectors' items. The edition consisted of 110 copies, 10 of which were special prints. Today, all are scarce.

The graphic works for the portfolios had been donated by renowned European artists to help the Bauhaus. The artistic élite of a whole generation were gathered together in this graphic rendezvous. Hopes of improving the financial position of the Bauhaus through sales of these portfolios were not, however, fulfilled, mainly because of the galloping inflation. The plan was to publish 5 portfolios, of which only 4 actually saw the light of day—numbers I, III, IV, and V. Moreover, number IV remained incomplete. Portfolio I contained 14 prints of works by the Bauhaus masters. Feininger had designed the title page—a delicate, flexible construction of interlaced letters of ethereal lightness. In addition, he provided 2 woodcuts, *Villa am Strand* (Villa on the Beach) and *Spaziergänger* (Strollers). He also designed the script of the title pages for the other portfolios. Portfolio II (which was never issued) was to have comprised works by artists of the French school. Portfolio III consists of 14 sheets by German artists who did not belong to the Bauhaus but were, in most cases, connected with the Sturm group. Portfolio IV, which was originally planned to contain 36 sheets, finally appeared with 11 works by Russian and Italian artists. Portfolio V contains 13 prints by German Expressionists.

But even during the Bauhaus period, Feininger regarded work on his own paintings, in the privacy of his studio, as more important than anything else. Hess's complete catalogue of his works dates 180 paintings between 1919 and 1933, of which 65 were done at Weimar (1919–24) and 109 at Dessau (1925–33). In 1933, Feininger painted only 6 pictures.

The artist's biographers have named several factors which had some bearing on the formation of his style: Cubism, the influence of Turner's paintings, and an affinity with the paintings of Caspar David Friedrich. Feininger came to know the Cubists in Paris and Turner's paintings on his visit to London. As to Friedrich's landscapes, he always maintained that they were completely unknown to him at the time when his style might have been influenced by them. Both Cubism and Futurism were responsible for the decisive change in Feininger's style. However, his utilization of pictorial space represents an individual solution of spatial problems which has nothing to do with analysis of form as interpreted by the Cubists. It would be quite wrong to describe his style as 'misunderstood Cubism', for one must assume that Feininger understood perfectly the Paris group's intentions of analytical reduction to basic forms. Nevertheless, he welcomed the formal elements discovered by the Cubists, using them as 'building bricks' for the development of his own style, but all the while moving farther away from Cubism on his own firmly individual path. Feininger's purpose was essentially different from that of the Cubists. They were attempting an objective definition—in the form of an equation—by the simultaneous representation of the different aspects of their subject in space and time; Feininger's aim was to make manifest the reflection in the human spirit of an object seen in meditation. To judge by Feininger's pictures, every landscape has its own 'beyond' in the background of our consciousness. The Cubists were theorists of perception; Feininger was a metaphysician. Thus, there is a fundamental difference in their way of looking at things, and Feininger's art patently belongs to German Expressionism, whose philosophy and vocabulary incline toward metaphysics. It is most important not to overlook or ignore this fact, since it shows that German Expressionism is firmly rooted in the tradition of German Romanticism. Feininger's pictures *Umpferstedt I* and *II* (Hess, Nos. 119, 120), of 1914, are still closely related to the Analytical Cubism of Picasso and Braque, in their rhythm, in their flocculent colour effects, and in their gradation of shades. Robert Delaunay's window pictures also come to mind. Although Feininger respected Delaunay as a painter, he rejected his Orphism as being too theoretical. By the time Feininger joined the Bauhaus, he had left direct dependence on Cubism far behind.

In Feininger's outlook, which was tinged with Romanticism, we find the explanation for his affinity with Caspar David Friedrich. Some of Feininger's seascapes bear a remarkable resemblance to those of Friedrich—not so much in style as in composition and in the glassy transparency of the colours. His *Wolken über dem Meer* (Clouds Over the Sea, Hess, No. 235), of 1923, brings to mind Friedrich's *Zwei Männer am Meer* (Two Men by the Sea), and *Wolken nach dem Sturm* (The Bird Cloud, Hess, No. 268), of 1926, is reminiscent of *Mönch am Meer* (Monk by the Sea); the present pays homage to the past. In both pictures, we have a meditative figure looking out over a low horizon toward a distance which suggests infinity. In each picture, the figure has the same weight in the composition, and even occupies the same place, with the same proportion in relation to the whole picture.

The relationship with Turner shows in Feininger's preoccupation with problems of light: representation of light by colour, the juxtaposition and interpenetration of warm and cold light zones, and the apparent power of light to dissolve matter.

In Feininger's pictures, time stands still. Movement is frozen into a moment of pure existence alone in space. In particular, the paintings dating from the Bauhaus period convey a sense of deep, solemn peace and transparent clarity. In this hush, ethereal vibration is created by columns of light oscillating between objects; this replaces the movement of matter and conveys a feeling of other-worldliness. An analysis of the components which produce this effect reveals architectonic motivation, musical analogies, and an attempt to express pure harmony of space by means of light and colour. These factors are balanced one against the other.

The architectural *Leitmotiv* is obvious. Architectural compositions take pride of place in Feininger's life's work. Out of a large number of pictures painted between 1919 and 1933, the following are of particular importance: *Eichelborn* (Hess, No. 208), of 1920; *Kirche von Mellingen* (Mellingen Church, Hess, No. 214), of the same year; *Torturm II* (Gate Tower II, Hess, No. 253), of 1925; and especially the different versions of *Gelmeroda*—VIII, of 1921 (Hess, No. 217); IX, of 1926 (Hess, No. 263); XI, of 1928 (Hess, No. 295); and XII, of 1929 (Hess, No. 311). These small Gothic churches of Thuringia were Feininger's means of illustrating his conception of the universal harmonic laws inherent in architecture. Here, perspective is not discarded but prismatically dissected. The buildings often look as though observed through a prism; the colour gradations enhance the illusion. There is an obvious reminder of Goethe's experiments with prisms in his *Farbenlehre* (theory of colour). Well-defined planes of colour in monochrome gradations are frequently superimposed—now translucent, now opaque, as if flowing together here, sharply separated there, reflecting light at one point, absorbing it at another. These buildings, with panels of glowing colour serving as walls, are composed of sharply defined rectangles, triangles, and polygons so angled, interlocked, and interpenetrating that they give the impression of real architecture—but architecture not subject to the laws of gravity.

This formal principle outgrows its starting point, namely the building depicted, and invades the complete surface of the pictorial space. The architecture of the church building calls for an architecture of the skies, which vanquishes the negative void of space. Figures too—appearing in diminutive size at the lower edge of the paintings—are involved in the vibration set up by this relationship. In *Gelmeroda IX*, the slowly walking group of monks who punctuate the foreground in a rhythmical sequence represent the sung responsory to the allegorical organ music of the whole composition. They resemble neumes (medieval musical notations), both in their individual shapes and in the varying levels of their heads.

The same technique of analysis and dissection can, indeed, be used for motifs other than architectural, and also appears in the representation of natural landscapes. *Das hohe Ufer* (The Bay, Hess, No. 234), of 1923, shows the coast of Fehmarn. The originality of Feininger's conception becomes all the more apparent when one compares it with Ernst Ludwig Kirchner's treatment of the same subject. The latter shows a steep, jagged coastline, overgrown with scrub and drawn with brusque, rapid strokes; in Feininger's work, absolute peace reigns over a massive, bare cliff formation devoid of vegetation, its tectonics strictly stylized in geometric forms. The almost sinister mood permeating the petrified landscape recalls the wide spaces in the pictures of the Italian metaphysicians of the Chirico and Carrà school. The two small figures by the water's edge seem to have turned to stone, and an oppressive sky broods over the earth. The air over the horizon rises up towards the sky, as if it were another, unreal mountain range, shaped like a pointed, glassy pyramid.

Again and again, one is forced to make comparisons with glasslike substances. In *Die blaue Insel* (The Blue Island, Hess, No. 362), of 1934, a glass ship sails over a glassy sea towards a glass mountain—the artist's island Erewhon, his Shangri-La, a fairy-tale. Writing in *Blickpunkt* (Vantage-Point, p. 134) about Feininger's studio in the Bauhaus, Georg Muche says:

> On the floor, leaning against the wall, were stacks of glass sheets of different sizes, which he needed for his frames. Standing one behind the other, vertical or horizontal, these right-angled, glassy-green, transparent planes had the same quality as the translucent element in his pictures. But this was only a coincidence; it was the crystal clear personality of their creator which was reflected in the form and content of the paintings.

An exceptional case is the *Glasscherbenbild* (Broken Glass, Hess, No. 280), of 1927, which shows different sizes of clear and coloured sheets of glass, ranged one behind the other, producing varied refractions. It looks as if the artist had tried to clarify his own formal alphabet. But such problems were very much in the air at the time; they were part of the *Zeitgeist*. To give but one example, Paul Scheerbart wrote in a brochure entitled *Glasarchitektur* (Glass Architecture), published by the Sturm as early as 1914:

> We mostly live in enclosed rooms. They are the environment for the growth of our civilization, which is, to a certain extent, the product of our architecture. If we want to raise it to a higher level, we needs must alter our architecture. To do this, we must put an end to the enclosed nature of the rooms in which we live, and this can only be achieved by the introduction of glass architecture which will let in the light of the sun, the moon and the stars, not only through a few windows, but through as many walls as possible, made entirely from glass—glass of different colours. This newly created environment will give us a new culture.

Allusion has been made to the significance of music in Feininger's painting. It is not intended to revive the trite metaphor of 'painted music'—the artist was not seeking to reproduce music in visual form. He wanted to find harmonic relationships in painting which, rising above technical differences, would be analogous to those in architecture and music. This idea is not Feininger's own invention, but recurs in the history of Expressionism and accompanies the evolution of abstract painting. Originally, it arose from the Romantic roots of Expressionism and received fresh impetus from the notion of the *Gesamtkunstwerk*, where all art forms are combined in supreme harmony. The very first abstract paintings by the Lithuanian M. K. Ciurlionis, dating from 1904, may be looked on as the visual equivalent of musical compositions. Kandinsky's abstract paintings equally presuppose a spiritual harmony of sound, colour, and form, and in the *Blaue Reiter Almanach* of 1912, he published an experimental stage-work where musical effects were to be superimposed. Similar experiments were also tried at the Bauhaus. Feininger, with his dual gifts as painter-musician, composed a series of fugues in 1922–23. In 1925, his *Fugue No. 6 in Three Voices for Organ and Piano* was published as a facsimile supplement to the *Europa Almanach* by Westheim and Einstein. Heinrich Neugeboren, a Bauhaus student, drafted two- and three-dimensional representations of a fugue from Bach's *Well-tempered Clavier.* Feininger's closest collaborator in the Bauhaus Press, Ludwig Hirschfeld-Mack, developed coloured light films initiated by Josef Hartwig and Kurt Schwertfeger, and one may assume that Feininger's work and ideas inspired him in this venture. Feininger's paintings, by the fugal and contrapuntal character of their form and colour, evoke strongly musical associations.

He was thus able to give visual representation to the pure harmony of space. When striking a tuning-fork, the hearer experiences the vibration as though the sound were hanging in space, until it dies away. Even the intensity of sound is experienced as spatial volume. A similar feeling is induced when looking at Feininger's landscape. The unfathomable expanse of space is made palpable and set into vibration by being dissected and organized into luminous bodies corresponding to sound vibrations. These luminous bodies are made visible as floating and interpenetrating, weightless, stereometric shapes—transparent or opaque, but clearly defined—and the manifold refraction of light results in the faceting of space, making finite its infinity, and endowing it with ever changing atmospheric qualities.

In addition to his paintings, Feininger did a large number of drawings and water-colours where he allowed free rein to his imagination which, for once, was not subjected to strict formal principles. In these, the atmosphere is not as calm as in his oil paintings; a finely drawn microcosm is bathed in a fluctuating, flowing light. Thinly drawn, broken contours barely hint at the subject rather than define it with precision. Quaint match-stick men and ghostly figures scurry across these wind-swept landscapes between crooked houses and decrepit three-masted ships.

The slogan 'Art and technology—a new unity' did not appeal to Feininger. He was convinced that these two concepts had nothing in common. When the Weimar Bauhaus came to an end, he agreed to move to Dessau only on condition that he would be relieved of his teaching duties. He kept his title of master, and lived in one of the masters' houses designed by Gropius at Dessau. He stayed with the Bauhaus until its very end in 1933. He left Germany in 1936, returning to America. He lived in New York until his death in January, 1956.

1. Feininger, Church at Niedergrundstedt, 1919—oil on canvas

2. Feininger, Mellingen V, 1917—India ink and water-colour

3. Feininger, Eichelborn, 1920—oil on canvas

4. Feininger, Upper Weimar VII, 1920—india ink and water-colour

5. Feininger, Small Mask, 1926—oil on canvas

6. Feininger, Pilgrimage Church in Erfurt I, 1924—oil on canvas

7. Feininger, Church Square, 1921—India ink and water-colour

8. Feininger, The Tower in Treptow, 1928—oil on canvas

9. Feininger, Yellow House and Small Figures, 1921—India ink and water-colour

10. Feininger, Blue Marine, 1924—oil on canvas

11. Feininger, Gelmeroda IX, 1926—oil on canvas

12. Feininger, Marine—Peppermint Harbour, 1929—oil on canvas

Ankunft der Motorsegler

22. 7. 30

13. Feininger, Arrival of the Motor Yachts, 1930—India ink and water-colour

14. Feininger, Cathedral Chancel, Halle, 1931—oil on canvas

15 a. Feininger,
The Bay, 1923—
oil on canvas

15 b. Feininger, Dalmatia,
1934—oil on canvas

16. Feininger, The Blue Island, 1934—oil on canvas

Feininger   das gestrandete Schiff   Freitag d. 30. VI. 22

17. Feininger, Beached Vessel, 1922—India ink and water-colour

18. Itten, The Red Tower, 1918—oil on canvas

JOHANNES ITTEN

Walter Gropius first met Johannes Itten in 1919 in Vienna, where the latter had founded a private art school. Gropius was interested in his teaching methods and, after discussing them with him, invited Itten to join the Bauhaus as a teacher. Itten accepted, and brought fourteen students with him from Vienna. At the Bauhaus, he instituted the *Vorkurs,* or basic course. This was an elementary art course compulsory for all first-year students. Endowed with considerable pedagogic insight and experience, Itten had developed a teaching method which released completely new creative potentialities in the student. It had the remarkable power of awakening artistic individuality, even where the imagination had become almost completely submerged. Itten's system has now, in somewhat diluted form, become an accepted method of art teaching. In many other fields of human endeavour it has pointed the way for the development of man's capacity for artistic expression and creativity.

The image of the Bauhaus in the first few years of its existence was, to a large extent, determined by Itten's colourful personality—a personality torn by a constant struggle to harmonize strong inner tensions. Of all the Bauhaus masters, Itten radiated the most intense personal aura. True, the powerful artistic authority of Kandinsky, Klee, and Schlemmer did not fail to exert an influence on the students, but this could not rival the fascination of Itten's intense and magnetic personality, which could either captivate or repel the students. He exerted a particularly strong attraction on the female students, inspiring in them a romantic exaltation. In 1919, Erika Tietze-Conrat, the art historian, wrote an article describing the teaching method at his school in Vienna. This was more in the nature of an apotheosis and ended in halting words of adoration. Even today, former Bauhaus students—now dear old ladies with grey hair—cannot speak of their former teacher without a dreamy expression coming into their eyes.

He did not escape criticism from his colleagues. 'I think I can see two ways in which Itten seeks to dominate', Schlemmer wrote to Otto Meyer-Amden in 1921. 'He is dictatorial and shows a complete lack of consideration for others. In addition, he indulges in a scholastic pedantry which drives the students to protest. (Schlemmer, *Briefe und Tagebücher* [Letters and Diaries], p. 195.) In old photographs, Itten stands before us like the guru of an esoteric sect, dressed in the monkish Bauhaus robe which he had designed himself and which was also worn by his assistant, Georg Muche; his skull is shaved, a wire frame with circular lenses perches on his nose, his hands are crossed, and a look of pious meditation is on his face. Yet, in spite of these affectations, there emerges the picture of a teacher of genius, but one whose remarkable ability was coupled with the intolerant arrogance sometimes found in a man fired by the missionary zeal of freshly discovered universal truths. Those who did not know him very well were inclined to ridicule Itten because of his idiosyncrasies, and there is no doubt that he was his own worst enemy. Nevertheless, this must not be allowed to obscure his great achievement in developing a teaching method which served to educate the imagination and to promote the harmonious development of the whole personality by integration of the body, mind, and spirit. Such an outlook is badly needed in our society's educational system, with its one-sided intellectual bias. Unfortunately, there is little sign that official teaching institutions have understood this need.

Like Klee, Itten was a native of the Bernese countryside. He was born at Südern-Linden, in Switzerland, on November 11, 1888. His father, a schoolmaster, died when he was four. Three years later, his mother, who was a farmer's daughter, married an Alpine highland farmer. 'At ten years of age, I was a perfect mountain-goat, though I could scarcely read or write', Itten says in his autobiography. From 1898 to 1904, he attended the grammar school at Thun. After he left school, his life entered on a checkered course. His aims were continually changing because of the versatility of the talents which, each striving for dominance, combined to fashion his wilful character. Equally gifted in the fields of art and science, he finally settled for a sphere of activity embracing both. From 1904 to 1908, he studied at the teachers' training college at Berne-Hofwil. His pedagogical insight was fostered by one of the more progressive members of the staff. He joined the Geneva *Ecole des Beaux Arts* in 1909, but he left after only one term, deeply disappointed. From 1910 to 1912, he studied mathematics and natural sciences at Berne University. On visits to Munich and Paris, he became acquainted with the art of the Blaue Reiter and Cubism. The influence of both is discernible in his style. At the conclusion of his university studies, he took a degree in teaching, and then decided to become a painter. Another brief period at the *Ecole des Beaux Arts* in Geneva only confirmed his previous conclusion that existing teaching methods were inadequate and out of date. At last, at the Stuttgart Academy of Art in 1913, he found his mentor, Adolf Hölzel, whose reputation rests on his achievements as a teacher and theoretician of art rather than on those as a painter. Hölzel was fiercely attacked by his colleagues at Stuttgart, who did not agree with his unacademic and unconventional teaching methods. In an atmosphere of unprecedented freedom, Hölzel fostered the individual gifts of his pupils. Like the Parisian Gustave Moreau, who preceded him by several decades, Hölzel is one of those fathers of modern art whose influence stems more from the work of their pupils than from their own. In addition to Itten, the circle of Hölzel pupils included Oskar Schlemmer, Willi Baumeister, Otto Meyer-Amden, and Ida Kerkovius. A lively exchange of artistic ideas and experiences developed between Baumeister, Schlemmer, and Itten during their Stuttgart years. Itten finally decided to adopt the career of art teacher after many discussions with Hölzel, who helped him with recommendations and advice. He went to Vienna in 1916, and two years later had collected a group of students who formed the nucleus of the first Itten school. In 1919, he dissolved the school and went to the Bauhaus.

Itten's work at the Bauhaus, which was often stormy and controversial, was governed by two guiding principles: Hölzel's educational theories, and the religious sect of Mazdaznan.

Like many educators, Itten was a believer in a 'system' and had a tendency to elevate his ideas into dogmas. The edifice of his teaching method was constructed with precision and strictly delineated. The vast store of ideas that he had made his own over the years was neatly classified and pigeon-holed. He had learned a great deal from his revered teacher Adolf Hölzel, mainly through conversation. It was Hölzel who trained him in the habit of tireless practice and firm artistic discipline. These methods, which he had found valid for his own work, he incorporated in his teaching. They earned him the reputation of pedantry.

Two of Hölzel's ideas that particularly impressed him were the problem of the picture as a two-dimensional construction, and the theory of colour. Hölzel had devised an elaborate theory of colour, which he demonstrated by means of coloured circles. This, too, owes a debt to Goethe's *Farbenlehre*, which was one of the major influences on the colour theories of German Expressionism. Itten worked out his own theory of colour, which went further than Hölzel's and was even more detailed. It is based on seven contrasting pairs: the contrasts of colour-in-itself, of light and dark, of cold and warm, the contrast between complementaries, simultaneous contrast, and qualitative and quantitative contrasts. In addition, there is Itten's own discovery: subjective colour values, deriving from the observation that every colour-sensitive person instinctively prefers colour combinations which accord with his personal and social circumstances.

On July 14, 1921, Schlemmer wrote to Otto Meyer-Amden:

As I told you, the Bauhaus kitchen is going to adopt the Mazdaznan diet. Itten and a few of his loyal supporters at the Bauhaus have been living according to its rules for some time, ever since Itten returned, full of enthusiasm, from a congress in Leipzig. He regards it as the only way to the creation of the new man, and he believes that a reform of habits of thought and feeling is essential before any progress can be made. In answer, I could only say that this close attention to the stomach, and to what passes our lips, would rob us of our spontaneity and make us forget the really important things such as the word and the spirit, and that I did not know that their purity depended on a pure stomach. . . . Itten wants to turn the Bauhaus into a monastery. From his pilgrimages to Beuron, I suspect that he has a similar organization in mind, for which I cannot refuse my reluctant admiration. What has become evident is that Itten, Muche, and a few faithful students have cut themselves off from the others to go their own way, which, with its exclusiveness, is intended both to proselytize and to set them apart. (Schlemmer, *Briefe und Tagebücher*, p. 116.)

At the end of World War I, a number of exclusive substitute religions sprang up in some European countries where the old social order was irretrievably in ruins. They offered people a refuge from the troubles of the world, promising them inner peace if they turned towards Oriental forms of belief. One of these sects was Mazdaznan. To the ancient Persian Mazdaism founded by Zarathustra had been added fragments from other Asiatic religions, refurbished for European consumption. The 'Mazdaznan Philosophy of Life' was founded by a German-American typographer, Otto Hänisch, born in Leipzig, who subsequently assumed the pseudonym of Dr Othomann Zar-Adusht Ha'nisch. It is a dualistic religion: the forces of light, led by Ahura Mazda, are engaged in a constant struggle for world supremacy against the forces of darkness, led by Angra Mainyu. It is man's duty to contribute towards the victory of the forces of light in the world. This can be achieved by his moral conduct, which liberates him from the forces of evil. He must refine his own being by expelling all gross matter from his body by means of fasting, a special vegetarian diet, purges, meditation, and breathing exercises, which restore his inner peace and free him from the rat-race of civilized society.

All this Itten tried to introduce into the Bauhaus. The catering became vegetarian, with results which are humourously described by one of the students, Paul Citroen: 'Everyone has a vegetarian look about him, that is to say, a pinched look of precarious "healthfulness".' (*Bauhaus Catalogue*, Frankfurt, 1964, p. 91.)

Moreover, each lesson of the basic course started with gymnastics, breathing, and loosening-up exercises. To find out what was going on, Paul Klee paid an unexpected visit to the basic course, which he described in a letter to his wife of January 16, 1921:

> After walking up and down once or twice, Itten heads towards an easel which holds a drawing board and a wad of sketching paper. He seizes a piece of charcoal, draws up his whole body as though charging it with energy, and then hurls himself at the easel. We now see, on the top sheet of paper, two forceful strokes, vertical and parallel, like this, and the students are requested to copy them. The master supervises the work, getting each student to demonstrate individually, while he controls the way they hold their bodies. Then he gives rhythmical commands while they repeat the exercise, and then everybody has to do the same exercise standing up. This is intended as a sort of body massage, to educate the machine to function by instinct. In a similar way, following his example, the students practise other elementary forms such as ⟨drawn symbol⟩, ⟨drawn symbol⟩ and ⟨drawn symbol⟩, with various explanations about the whys and wherefores. Then he talks about a storm; some of the students have to stand up and demonstrate how they experience wind and storm. The next thing is a representation

of a storm, for which he allows about ten minutes, and then inspects the results. Whereupon he holds a critical session. After the criticism, they return to work. One sheet of paper after another is torn off and falls to the floor. Some of the students work with such vigour that several sheets are ripped off together and go to waste. When they are all tired out, he dismisses them, but not without getting them to take the exercise home for further practice. (Itten, *Mein Vorkurs am Bauhaus* [My Basic Course at the Bauhaus], p. 17.)

However bizarre this kind of teaching may have appeared for an art academy, it was not as far-fetched as would seem. Itten did not want to turn out merely expert practitioners whose art was calculated to conform to rules. His first aim was to set people free from their inhibitions, to loosen them up and to heal the wounds inflicted by civilization. Only then would they be receptive to art education as such. He therefore began the lessons with physical training sessions. The limbering-up exercises were intended to make the students aware of their own bodies and of the movements through which their hands projected the form of a picture onto a surface. To a generation familiar with Jackson Pollock's action painting, this sounds quite reasonable.

Itten wanted to lead his students towards artistic experience by way of feeling rather than intellect. Reproductions of old masters were used in the basic course for analysis by the students. However, the usual form of analysis by intellectual dissection was taboo—they were expected to project their emotions into the picture. The feelings thus aroused would then be committed to paper in terms of light and dark contrasts, distribution of mass, rhythms, lines of composition, or other factors suggested by the picture. At these sessions, too, dramatic incidents were not uncommon. In 1921, Schlemmer wrote to Meyer-Amden:

At Weimar, Itten teaches analysis. He shows slides to the students who then have to draw certain essential elements, say, movement, the main line, a curve. ... He shows a Gothic figure, and then the weeping Magdalen from the Grünewald Altar. The students are working hard to extract the essence of this very complicated composition. Itten watches their fumblings, and roars: If you had any kind of artistic sensibility, you would not sit there drawing in the face of this sublime representation of tears— the sorrow of the world—you would be dissolved in tears yourselves! With these words, he rushes out, slamming the door behind him. (Schlemmer, *Briefe und Tagebücher*, p. 112.)

The special intelligence of the artist is distinguished from that of ordinary mortals by clearer insight in the realm of the imagination. This is the result of a refinement of the organs of perception, brought about by heightened sensitivity and precision of the feelings. Only constant, repeated practice sharpens the sensibilities and prevents them from becoming blunted. This is what Itten had in mind for his pupils with his limbering-up exercises and rhythmic-movement studies, as well as his classification of opposing qualities of perception into contrasting pairs, to be experienced by the students, reproduced in expressive gestures, and put down on paper in the form of sketches and drawings. A great many studies were composed with contrasting accents—black and white, light and dark gradations, large and small, high and low, and the like—never losing sight of the aspect of rhythmic distribution within the picture.

Itten also wanted to educate the sense of touch, to increase its sensitivity and perceptivity. This led to his invention of the study of materials. Fabric remnants and oddments of the most diverse materials with different surface structures and textures were collected and combined into more or less intriguing constructions. Glass, wood, metals, fabrics, furs, feathers, shavings— these were all assembled into imaginative structures. These heterogeneous combinations high-lighted the contrasting properties of the materials: the smoothness and transparency of glass, the grain of wood, the fibre and roughness of fabrics, the gleam and sparkle of metals, and so on.

Itten's reputation rests on his teaching achievements rather than on his painting. He can hardly be called a painter in the usual sense of the word; it would be more correct to describe him as a philosopher of form, expressing on canvas his intuitive perceptions.

At first sight, Itten's artistic development seems to be inconsistent, but on closer examination, the opposite proves to be the case. It follows a clear evolutionary curve, starting with abstraction, and proceeding through Cubism to a study of nature and the faithful representation of landscape. From there, it passes through various stages of stylization of the object, finally to return to the starting point—strict abstraction. His first pictures were painted in 1915 and were shown at the Sturm Gallery in Berlin the following year. The works completed between 1915 and 1917 are characterized by a somewhat complex rhythm in the division of space. Only their vivid colours are inspired by Hölzel; their form represents a free adaptation of Cubism. The triangle, the rectangle, and the circle are constantly recurring elements which Itten blended into articulated 'chords' or harmonies expressing the attunement of his inner self.

In 1918, Itten discovered the significance of automatism in artistic creation, achieved by shutting off all intellectual control during the creative process. The aim was to paint intuitively, without, however, falling into a trance. Meditation lies at the core of his conception of artistic experience, and his earlier works reveal their meaning most fully when they are observed with the conscious mind 'switched off'.

In addition to purely abstract forms, some of Itten's paintings depicted objects in a representational manner, revealing an individual style of Romantic Cubism. Examples of this are: *Der Oratoriensänger* (The Oratorio Singer) and *Häusergruppe im Frühling* (Group of Houses in Spring—Stuttgart, Killesberg), of 1916; and *Der rote Turm* (The Red Tower) and *Ländliches Fest* (Rural Gaiety), painted in 1918 and 1919. As was the case with Feininger, Itten was stimulated by Cubism, but his own interpretation of it diverged considerably from that of the French school. Like Feininger, Itten was a metaphysician, not a theoretician of perception. He sought a vision rather than an objective analysis; his search was for the inner landscape, or 'inscape', not for a penetrating analysis of the outside world. The here-and-now was confronted by the beyond. Descartes was answered by Jakob Böhme; the West by the East. Itten described his years at the Bauhaus as 'Universalist', rejecting the epithet of 'Romantic'. His characteristic colour schemes—bright, shining reds, warm ultramarine blues, strong yellows, and mother-of-pearl whites—recall those of the Blaue Reiter, particularly Marc, Macke, Campendonk, and Kandinsky. In 1919, Itten did a series of nude drawings, stylized and Expressionist in character. During the Bauhaus period, he did very little painting, as he was too involved in educational activities. The most notable works of that time were landscape drawings, in which he endeavoured to capture the essence of natural scenes in shades of black and white.

The most important painting dating from Itten's Bauhaus period, his *Kinderbildnis* (Portrait of a Child), of 1922, is a statement of his human and artistic creed. It is a magical picture, with all sorts of magic formulae built in. Its calculated formalism imparts to the composition an odd feeling of deliberate remoteness. The painting is reminiscent of fourteenth-century pictures. This is due not only to the clashing perspectives, but also to the direct confrontation of structures on varying levels of reality. Against a bright background, one perspective leads towards the centre of the picture from a wall of realistically simulated woodgrain, supported by a column. This is in apparent contrast to the rippling rows of coloured bands laid without perspective flat on the floor. In this picture, Itten applied his theory of perception contrasts. The rigid, distant expression on the child's face resembles fourteenth-century representations of the Christ-child. On his head, the child wears a strange crown-shaped hat, a sort of inspirational cap. Behind him, a flowering shrub looks as though it were growing out of his body—the tree of life. On the left, the concealed door of the house of the world; on the right, a cube—the small house of terrestrial personality; between them, coloured waves—the paths of life. Top right, a circle enclosing a six-pointed star made up of interlocking triangles contains a mandala symbol—a person's divine diagram. Within the circle, a jumbled arrangement of letters forms the phrase *Ave Ahura Masda*. Below the mandala circle, the child's name appears on a floating scroll, 'Johann-Matthias Itten'. The child—the artist's son—is surrounded by symbols of his status. Spheres, cubes, circles, squares, and triangles appear repeatedly. At the child's feet lies a ball casting a shadow—terrestrial reflection of the mandala, or embodiment of the spirit. In his left hand, the child holds a cube—symbol of the terrestrial; in his right, a clock—symbol of the temporal. All of this establishes the formal and transcendental connections between mandala and ball, between celestial and terrestrial vocation. At the right, on the cube house, stands a board with coloured squares—the colour horoscope which the artist devised for his son in accordance with his doctrine.

In 1923, Itten left the Bauhaus, following disagreements with Gropius. The latter felt he could no longer take responsibility for Itten's activities. Itten, on his part, found that the Bauhaus was no longer a suitable field for him. Gropius continued along the path of social communication; Itten along that of contemplation. He spent the next three years at the Mazdaznan School of Life at Herrliberg near Zürich. In 1926, he moved to Berlin where he founded his own school of art, at which Mordechai Ardon, later to become known as the major Israeli painter, also taught. From 1932 to 1938, he taught at the Krefeld School of Textile Design. In 1938, he was appointed director of the School of Applied Arts in Zürich. He continued to live in Zürich until has death in 1967.

19. Itten, Portrait of a Child, 1922—oil on panel

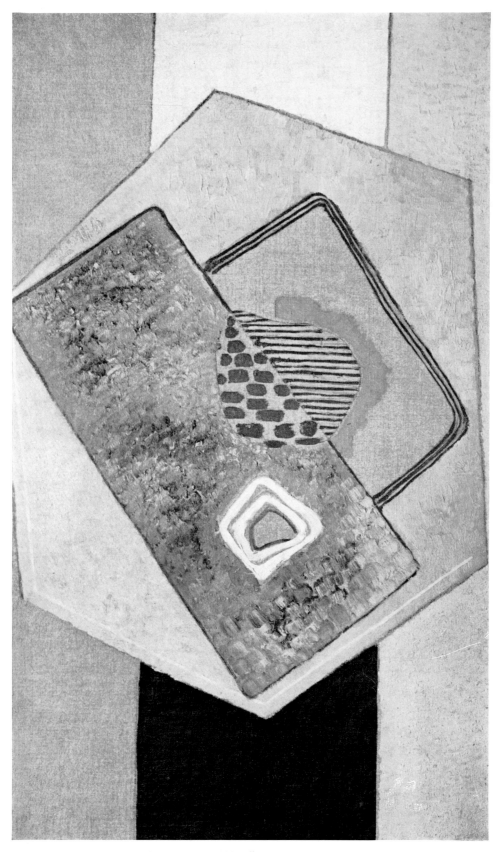

20. Muche, Grey-Blue-Pink Composition, 1921—oil on canvas

GEORG MUCHE

Georg Muche was the youngest of the Bauhaus masters. In 1920, when Muche was twenty-five, Gropius appointed him on the recommendation of Muche's older friend Johannes Molzahn, who belonged to the Sturm circle. Muche's artistic vision had a great deal in common with Molzahn's; their abstract forms were ciphers in an autonomous realm of the spirit. In a sense, therefore, Muche's painting can be described as metaphysical. At first, both Muche and Molzahn regarded the Bauhaus program with scepticism. 'The ideas of Ruskin, Morris and the German Werkbund left us cold', Muche wrote in *Blickpunkt* (p. 163). 'Nothing was more remote from our minds than the medievalism of the *Bauhütte* [medieval craft guild] which one could read between the lines of the Bauhaus manifesto.' However, when Feininger told him about the students' youthful enthusiasm, and when Itten showed him round an exhibition of works by students of the basic course, Muche was won over. He and Itten became close friends.

During the years that followed, up to Itten's departure, Muche worked as his assistant on the basic course, made Itten's ideas his own, and deputized for him in his absence. His temperament was the very opposite of Itten's: quiet and conciliatory, he often acted as mediator between his missionary friend, who was scintillating with ideas, and the student body. Rather than impose his own views on the students, Muche taught with patience and understanding, by coaxing out each individual talent and by helping each student to follow the path most suitable for him. Group photographs show Muche among his colleagues as a tall, slim young man with blond hair and a reserved manner.

He took over the artistic direction of the Bauhaus weaving shop, though he could not muster much enthusiasm for it. The women students based some of their textile patterns on his designs, but he wrote in *Blickpunkt* (p. 168): 'I promised myself never to design a textile pattern with my own hands as long as I lived. I have kept this promise. I wanted to hold myself in readiness for painting because I knew that one day it would come back to me.' He had little aptitude for the technical and business aspects of the workshop, to which he attended only as a matter of duty.

On June 17, 1925, Schlemmer wrote to his wife: 'On Saturday night, Muche arrived from Berlin on a lorry with seven weaving looms he had bought there. Poor Gunda [Gunta Stölzl] was horrified to hear how much he had paid for them. Muche says he is fed up with being a businessman, and grumbles about his work.' (Schlemmer, *Briefe und Tagebücher*, p. 168.)

Georg Muche was born on May 8, 1895, at Querfurt, a small town in the brown-coal area of central Germany. He grew up in the Rhön mountain district. His father, Felix Muche, a minor official, one day suddenly began to paint. With his sentimental idylls, he soon made a name for himself as a self-taught, German primitive. He adopted the pseudonym of Ramholz, which was the name of his village. While still at grammar school, Georg discovered his own passion for painting. The idea of abstract painting came as a sudden revelation to him one evening when he was passing a field of yellow flowering rape, bathed in the unreal light of the evening sky—a vision similar to Kandinsky's sudden vision a generation before him. In 1913, Muche began to study art at the Academy in Munich, where he visited the Blaue Reiter exhibition at the Hans Goltz Gallery. Here, he saw his own ideas confirmed and anticipated in pictures created by painters as old as his father. At the exhibition, he got into conversation with Marianne von Werefkin, who introduced him to Alexei Jawlensky and Kandinsky. Muche studied in Munich until 1915, when he painted his first abstract composition. He made the acquaintance of Herwarth Walden, and showed his paintings in the latter's Sturm Gallery in 1916. He also taught at the Sturm School of Art in Berlin. In 1917–18, he served as a soldier in France, where his early heroic enthusiasm soon gave way to disillusionment. On his return from the war, he again went to Berlin where he stayed until his move to Weimar.

The development of Muche's style starts from abstraction and ends with representation. Between these two extremes, there is a series of small though clearly distinguishable stylistic metamorphoses. However, all his works have some characteristic features in common: they bear the imprint of his own personality—unobtrusive, reticent, and delicate, with a subtle effect which may make little immediate impact but is none-the-less enduring. Even his blond hair seems to be reflected in the pale tones he uses. His compositions hover between sky and earth. He seems to be in constant fear of being lifted off the ground to disappear in space, and to be trying to counter this impulse towards ethereal dissolution with the opposing force of earthly gravity. This is why all his works, whether representational or not, seem to maintain only a precarious balance. At times, one almost feels as if a pendulum has only just come to rest. Muche's formal principles are linear tension and organized areas of colour nuances.

Muche's vision of the field of yellow rape dominated his early abstract works. 'So they [the artists of the Blaue Reiter] had discovered a new world! I envied them and at the same time realized that, to make discoveries myself, I must not search for them in abstraction. But I still wanted to paint fields forming rectangles, and the shimmering grey of the sky beneath which flowers the glowing rape.' (Muche, *Blickpunkt*, p. 220.)

The construction of his first paintings was rather heavy, as in *Komposition mit dunklem Grund* (Composition with Dark Background) and *Das grosse Bild XX* (Picture XX), both painted in 1916. In these paintings, broad, black ridges intersect, forming corners and angles and dividing the surface into segments, rectangles, and triangles, giving it the appearance of a jigsaw puzzle. A short while later, Muche's division of the pictorial space becomes lighter, more delicate, and more flexible. *Das Bild mit Gittermotiv* (Picture with Trellis Motif), of 1919, is one of a series of paintings in which checkered panels of differing weight, opacity, and size are dovetailed to form a mobile screen. This gives the impression of a bas-relief, the colours of which appear to have been disposed as if through a sieve. In his paintings of 1920, the trellis motif appears again, but, in addition, Muche tackles new problems. In *Komposition mit schwarzer und grüner Form* (Composition with Black and Green Forms), an illusion of space has been achieved by an apparently cylindrical roll formed by the trellised object in the centre. In *Bild mit schwebendem Rot* (Picture with Floating Red), the cohesion of the trellised structure is burst asunder by a puffy explosion of red from the centre. Representation of the object is here foreshadowed by the presence of small forms suggesting figures. In both of these paintings, the colours are light and glowing, with a mother-of-pearl iridescence, roughly grained and often merging into each other.

During his years at the Bauhaus, pressure of other work prevented Muche from doing much painting. His few works of that period include *Bild mit Hand* (Picture with Hand), of 1920, *Komposition in Graublau-Rosa* (Grey-Blue Pink Composition), of 1921, and *Zwei Eimer* (Two Buckets), of 1923. In these formalized still-lifes, he embarked upon the representation of objects of simple shape. In form and colour, he adopted a Synthetic Cubism which calls to mind the works of Juan Gris, Jean Metzinger, and Albert Gleizes.

The *Bild mit Hand* has a ghostly effect. On the left-hand side, in front of a wall divided into advancing and receding sections, stands a burning candle which casts a sharply outlined shadow towards the right. To the right of the shadow, a translucent panel seems to protrude diagonally from the wall. It is not clear whether this is suspended in the air or fixed to the wall. The shimmering phosphorescence could come from within the panel or could equally well be a reflection of candle-light. On it, a green hand has left its imprint, like a silent *Mene Tekel*, an emanation from the beyond. Muche describes a visit to his Weimar studio by Joseph Strzygowski, the art historian, who tried to interpret the meaning of the hand: 'This hand points towards the Far East, although I doubt whether your inspiration came from this direction. I believe it came from North Africa. It is probably the hand of Fatima [Muhammed's daughter].' (Muche, *Blickpunkt,* p. 137.) After several hours' reflection, Muche finally remembered a war-time experience which had been buried in his subconscious. Early one summer's morning, on the Somme, he had found a tattered piece of cloth—the lost standard of a North African cavalry regiment. It showed a white hand on a green background. This anecdote throws light on his working method. His work is done in a state of meditation but subject to a conscious control which acts as a filter on his imagination. Thus the image of the hand had changed colour as it returned to the mind's eye years later. The white hand on a green background had turned into a green hand against a light background. A variation of the same motif appears in Muche's etching *Hand mit zwei Herzen über Schachbrett* (Hand with Two Hearts on Chessboard), of 1921, one of the works in the first Bauhaus portfolio.

In 1922, Muche painted several pictures of plant life. The individual plants are not quite tangible; their outlines merge with their shadows in a fluid halo. In the fluctuating light, it is sometimes difficult to distinguish the solid from its shadow. A mystic life-force pervades the luxuriant vegetation of fungi, mosses, ferns, leaves, and blossoms growing in the warm, damp humus that has formed between earth and sky. In this mysterious atmosphere, the breath of fertility gently sways the pullulating undergrowth. In the same year, Muche painted a *Kinderkopf* (Child's Head), embedded in elements of vegetation, from which the pale profile emerges almost as a young bird breaking out of its eggshell. In this picture, the human being is still enveloped by elemental growth forms, but from 1923 onwards, the human figure is given more prominence. In these later pictures, Arcadian beings regard us with a quiet, relaxed self-assurance.

Muche's style in painting gives no clue to his active interest in the architectural field which was awakened at the Bauhaus. Muche never studied architecture, and his colleagues must have been surprised when he unexpectedly began to design dwelling-houses, down to the last detail. Gropius gave him a free hand. As a self-taught architect, Muche displayed an astonishing sureness of touch. He made a valuable contribution to the Bauhaus exhibition of 1923. His 'model house' was shown as a representative example of the architectonic spirit of the Bauhaus. The soundness of Muche's idea of building mass-produced houses from prefabricated parts has long since been borne out by experience. At the time, it went no further than the single model house which was erected in Weimar. In 1924, Muche went on a study trip to the United States, where the modern architecture made a strong impression on him. Following his return, he designed the prototype of a metal house at Dessau in 1926, which was actually built. His use of new materials was intended to bring about a reduction in weight and to make the building more easily transportable, capable of extension, and adaptable to different uses.

Muche's two major interests reflect the ambiguity inherent in the Bauhaus program. He reacted with signs of a dual personality: Muche, the painter, is not the same person as Muche, the architect. Painting has no useful purpose but is meaningful—therefore it is art; architecture has a functional rationale—therefore it is technology. This is why he, too, rejected the slogan 'Art and technology—a new unity', and kept both firmly apart. In an article entitled *Kunst und Technik—eine neue Einheit* (Fine Art and Industrial Forms), Muche wrote:

> Art and technology are not a new unity. There is an essential difference in their artistic values. The limits of technology are circumscribed by reality, whereas the criterion of art is the striving towards the ideal. In the realm of art, opposites form a whole. Transcending technical considerations, art is created in the utopia of its own reality. *(Bauhaus: Zeitschrift*

21. Muche, Two Buckets, 1923—oil on canvas

22. Muche, Four Accents, 1920—oil on canvas

23. Muche, Composition with Black and Green Forms, 1920—oil on canvas

24. Muche, Withering Plants, 1922—oil on canvas

für Bau und Gestaltung [Bauhaus: Building and Construction Publication], Vol. I, No. 1, Dessau, 1926.)

This quotation indicates one of the reasons for Muche's eventual departure. Nevertheless, unlike his friends Itten and Schreyer, he decided to move to Dessau where he remained until the beginning of 1927, but with the gradual change in atmosphere that occurred at Dessau, he became increasingly unhappy and felt out of place there. On July 11, 1926, he made the following note:

> It is terrible for me here. If I did not make a conscious effort all the time to keep going, I would become very depressed. There can no longer be any doubt that I shall leave here in April. Would it were today! I am most profoundly alienated from everything and almost everybody. This is not to say that working conditions and human relations are unsatisfactory, but the fact is that I can no longer identify myself with the Bauhaus because of my aims and ideas, however vague they may be at the moment. I am unutterably bored, and in these circumstances, a neutral environment must be better for me.

And on February 18, 1927, he concluded an observation with the remark: 'I don't want to grow old with Kandinsky and Klee—nor even with Moholy.' (Muche, *Blickpunkt*, p. 170.)

In 1927, Muche moved to Berlin, where he taught at Itten's school of art. From 1931 to 1933, he was a professor at the State Academy of Art, Breslau, until it was closed by the government. In the meantime, his style had become completely representational, but with certain Surrealist elements, which transformed his scenes into dream landscapes. Presentiments of the approaching catastrophe were expressed in crowd scenes showing the multitudes quietly and patiently awaiting the inevitable apocalypse. In Breslau, he started to do extensive fresco studies. His later frescoes at Krefeld were destroyed during an air raid in 1943. From 1934–38, he taught at the Kunst und Werk School of Hugo Häring. From 1939 to 1959, he was head of the senior class at the Krefeld School of Textile Design. He also collaborated with Baumeister and Schlemmer at the Wuppertal Institute of Painting Materials in 1942. Muche now lives at Lindau on the Bodensee.

LOTHAR SCHREYER

Lothar Schreyer taught at the Bauhaus from 1920 to 1923. He was a mystic, born in Saxony like the early seventeenth-century mystic and philosophical theologian Jakob Böhme, who had a great influence on his thinking. During the few years Schreyer spent at the Bauhaus, his own uncompromising idealism was one of the forces that helped to fashion Bauhaus philosophy. But when he finally left, he had come to realize that his artistic views were, after all, fundamentally too different to accomodate to the Bauhaus rationale.

Many an artist is a priest manqué. Both share a tendency to introspection coupled with a need for communication. What distinguishes the artist from the priest, however, is the outward form in which he expresses his creed: not through the traditional rites of the Church but through symbols of his own invention. This applies particularly to Itten, Muche, and Schreyer, all of whom felt a longing for monastic retreat after leaving the Bauhaus. Perhaps as a reaction from teaching and preaching, they displayed a pronounced desire for seclusion.

Gropius brought Schreyer to the Bauhaus after seeing his work at the Kampf Theatre in Hamburg where Schreyer was the director. Gropius was impressed by his method of stage production and asked him to take over the theatre workshop at the Bauhaus. Schreyer's masques were precursors of Schlemmer's ballet, although they arose from totally different concepts. Schreyer was an Expressionist, and used the literary and artistic language of Expressionism to give a twentieth-century interpretation to basic human experience and the unchanging tenets of Christianity. He regarded the theatre as a sacred rite, a religious mystery play. The final logic of his endeavours to symbolize aspects of human destiny through ritual figures led to the complete depersonalization of his characters, who became mere prototypes, projected into stage sets and actions charged with occult meanings, which were expressed in a kind of demonic grammar. His work never found acceptance by a wider public: it was too difficult to understand, too introspective. By the attempt to reduce existence to its bare bones, the productions became esoteric in the extreme.

In a draft dated October 20, 1922, which was intended as a contribution to a brochure on the Bauhaus Theatre, Walter Gropius wrote: 'In its very origins, the stage arose from man's religious yearnings (Theatre = seeing God). Its task is to make manifest a transcendental idea. Therefore, its impact on the soul of the spectator and hearer is dependent on its success in translating the idea into the realms of perception (optical and auditory).' (Wingler, *Bauhaus*, p. 72.) In these lines, Gropius made himself the mouthpiece of Schreyer's beliefs.

Lothar Schreyer was born on August 19, 1886, at Blasewitz, near Dresden. He studied art history and law at the universities of Heidelberg, Berlin, and Leipzig. After graduating in law, he found he was more interested in art. He began to draw, to paint, to write poetry, and he formulated his ideas for a renaissance of the stage. In 1912, he became producer at the German Theatre in Hamburg. At the beginning of the war, he visited Herwarth Walden in Berlin. They took an immediate liking to each other, and soon became close collaborators. Schreyer had his poems published in the Sturm magazine, and he deputized for the editor from time to time. He founded the Sturm Theatre, where experimental Expressionist plays were performed by actors of Herwarth Walden's circle. Their first play—*Santa Susanna*, by August Stramm—was presented to the public in the autumn of 1918. As a result of the troubles in Berlin after the war, the Sturm Theatre moved to Hamburg, where Schreyer was living, and changed its name to Kampf Theatre in 1919.

The following plays were produced at the Kampf Theatre: *Die Heidebraut* and *Kräfte*, by August Stramm; *Der Tod des Empedokles* (Death of Empedocles), by Hölderlin; *Sünde* (Sin), a drama by Herwarth Walden; and a nativity play based on an old German text. Schreyer's own plays were entitled *Kindsterben* (Child's Death), *Mann* (Man), and *Kreuzigung* (Crucifixion). The text for these plays was quite unlike an ordinary dramatic script. It was more like a musical score, written in hieroglyphic symbols invented by Schreyer, incorporating grammalogues, figure symbols, lines of music, notations of tempo, rhythm, and the like. A scenario for Schreyer's *Kreuzigung* was published in a limited edition which is now a very rare item of Expressionist drama. It is a large, broadside volume, itself a work of art in which the woodcuts and colours applied by stencil were contributed by Max Billert and Max Olderock. The introduction to *Kreuzigung* reads as follows:

> The reader of this scenario must know: The creation of this plan and the symbols in which it is written are as significant for the stage as was the creation of musical notation for music. Anyone can read this plan who is capable of hearing the sound of the words within himself and of seeing coloured form in movement.

> The actor who uses this scenario must know: This plan can be acted only by one who is not a professional actor, who does not make a living out of the theatre, who is not a critic, and who does not want *himself*. Anyone can act this plan who can see himself, hear himself, stand outside himself, who follows the plan without reservations, and who lives in community with the other players.

> Those who hear and see the scenario must know: The play can only be seen and heard in a circle of friends as a common experience, as a common act of devotion, as a common creation.

The wording of this introduction reveals the fervour of the period. Implicit in the text is the ideal of the *Gesamtkunstwerk*, embodied in the community of players who are expressly instructed, as is the audience, that the play can only be comprehended through empathy, not by the intellect. As in the work of other Bauhaus masters, the basic conception is one of synaesthesia, based on the idea that colour, sound, and speech can communicate equivalent experiences through different means of perception.

Schreyer's poetic language comes closest to that of August Stramm. It dispenses with syntax and the logic of grammar, in order to revert to the original meaning of vocal sounds; it is thus onomatopoetic and evocative. It aims at reproducing the pure, spontaneous, unbroken utterance of the soul, which lies between music and speech—the scream, the sob, the entreaty, singsong, stammered speech.

It is very difficult to find one's way about Schreyer's edifice of ideas, either as spectator or as actor. Masks, not people, are needed to give voice to his Orphic word-archetypes. The chorus of antiquity is reduced to a single demonic individual. It is he—not the hero—who takes the lead; it is the Furies—not Oedipus—who dominate the action. The theatre has reverted to a pre-Hellenic stage. Therefore, the actor must become detached from his own individuality and lose himself in anonymity. Schreyer's choreographic directions are designed to let the action of the play unfold through expressive ceremonial dances. In these, the figures, with their masks and stereotyped movements, behave like puppets. The general effect is enhanced by the musical accompaniment with instruments such as tom-toms and musical glasses which, with their monotonous rhythms and eerie sounds, evoke the mood of an exorcism of spirits. Taking his ideas to their logical conclusion, Schreyer wrote a puppet play, *Geburt* (Birth). He designed the costumes for all his characters, down to the minutest detail, in exquisite water-colours. Contrasts of black, red, green, yellow, and white predominate in his colour schemes. In spite of the Christian content of Schreyer's stage works, the figurines look like exotic idols, and indeed they are intended to have a magical effect. They are reminiscent of South Sea Island carvings or totem figures of Indian tribes of the northwest coast of America.

Schreyer's interpretation of art as magic ritual led him to build shrines for the dead. The *Totenhaus der Frau* (Death House of Woman) and the *Totenhaus des Mannes* (Death House of Man) were sarcophagi which were intended to sanctify not only the souls of the deceased but also their bodies. He made the *Totenhaus des Mannes* in Weimar; its lid was decorated with the painting *Totenbild des Mannes* (Death Picture of Man). This was a composition of Cubist abstraction, showing a severely religious figure with the sign of the Cross on his forehead—a Christian-Expressionist picture of a mummy. As a constant *memento mori*, it hung on the wall of Schreyer's studio next to the *Totenbild der Frau* (Death Picture of Woman).

In March, 1923, Schreyer produced his own *Mondspiel* (Moon Play) on the Bauhaus stage. It was a complete disaster, rejected by masters and students alike. Schreyer's highly pitched Expressionism was completely at odds with the general trend of Bauhaus feeling. Following this fiasco, Schreyer left the Bauhaus. The theatre workshop was taken over by Schlemmer. From 1924 to 1927,

25. Schreyer, Man—water-colour and India ink

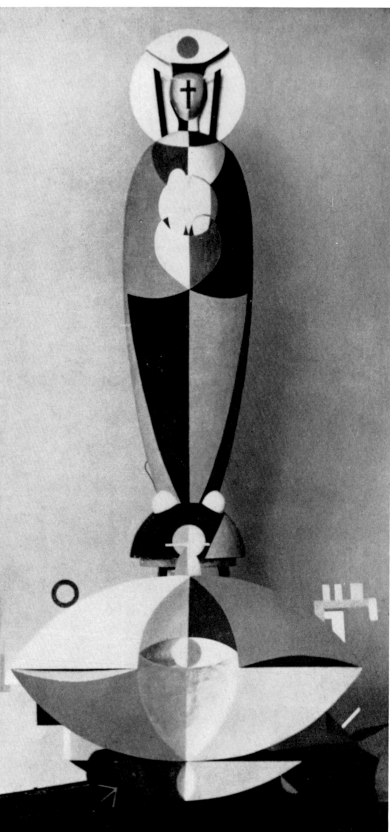

26 a. Schreyer, Death Picture of Man for the Death House of Man, 1920—painted wood

26 b. Schreyer, Virgin in the Moon;
at her Feet the Dancer
with the Dance Shield—mask

Schreyer taught at the Weg School in Dresden. He subsequently published a number of works about Christian art, about the Sturm and the Bauhaus. In 1927, he returned to Hamburg, where he died in 1966.

Itten, Muche, and Schreyer were a trio of prophets representing an inward-looking way of life which found its particular expression in art. All three refused to believe that art and technology could be brought under a common denominator. They are representatives of the Weimar period, protagonists of an alternative Bauhaus philosophy which never achieved acceptance.

OSKAR SCHLEMMER

Oskar Schlemmer came to the Bauhaus in December, 1920. Gropius' offer of a post reached him in the middle of his work on sets and costume designs for the première of Kokoschka's *Mörder—Hoffnungen der Frauen* (Murderers, Hopes of Women) and *Das Nusch-Nuschi* by Franz Blei at the Stuttgart State Theatre. Schlemmer was also toying with the idea of moving to Dresden or Darmstadt, and he accepted Gropius' offer only reluctantly. In his letters and diaries, which his wife published after his death, Schlemmer drew a lively picture of life and work at the Bauhaus both in Weimar and Dessau. An entry of December, 1920, reads: 'Should I call it off at the last minute? Turn down my vocation? Some would say it is madness; others would disagree. Advantages—disadvantages.' (Schlemmer, *Briefe und Tagebücher*, p. 97.)

These words betray an irresolute character, and this difficulty in making up his mind often hampered Schlemmer in his career. But on December 21, 1920, he wrote to his friend Otto Meyer-Amden: 'Weimar: the contract has been signed from January 1 to April 1.' (Schlemmer, *Briefe und Tagebücher*, p. 103.) However, before finally settling down in Weimar, he traveled back and forth between Stuttgart and his new place of work for some time.

His first appointment was as 'Master of Form' in charge of the stone sculpture workshop, but in May, 1923, when Schreyer left after his *Mondspiel* fiasco, Schlemmer took over the theatre workshop. His Triadic Ballet had received its first performance at Stuttgart the year before. Oskar Schlemmer's theatrical mission proved to be his most significant contribution to the Bauhaus.

In 1922, Schlemmer designed the final form of the Bauhaus emblem—a stylized profile within a circle. But he left his mark on the profile of the Bauhaus in more ways than one—all of his intensive artistic activities contributed to its physiognomy. In contrast to Itten, Muche, and Schreyer, he saw no fundamental discrepancy between art and technology. His outlook helped to preserve the continuity of the Bauhaus spirit when the move was made from Weimar to Dessau.

On essential points, Schlemmer's artistic views were in agreement with those of most of his colleagues at the Bauhaus, although there were, of course, a number of differences of opinion. He was a metaphysician, and in his search for analogies to his own ideas, he turned to German Romanticism in different media of expression. The ideal conception of the *Gesamtkunstwerk* was implicit in all his work. In painting, Schlemmer could project on to the two-dimensional-plane problems with which he was concerned in other disciplines—sculpture, the dance, theatrical production, and costume and stage design. The imaginary space and movement of his paintings capture the three-dimensional choreography of the stage.

Schlemmer often used the words 'metaphysics' and 'metaphysical'. An entry in his diary of November, 1922, says: 'There remains the metaphysical—in other words, Art' (Schlemmer, *Briefe und Tagebücher,* p. 144.), and, speaking of dance, he mentioned 'the metaphysics which dwell within the human body' and 'exact metaphysics'. (Schlemmer, *Abstraktion in Tanz und Kostüm* [Abstraction in Dance and Costume], 1928.)

As a painter, Schlemmer leaned to German Romanticism, particularly Philip Otto Runge, to whom he often referred. During a discussion in May, 1922, he strongly resisted the suggestion that if Runge had lived a century later he would have been opposed to the Bauhaus. In November, 1924, he wrote: 'I very much like this sentence of Runge's: "Strict regularity is most necessary of all, especially in works of art without a historic content, which arise straight from the imagination of our souls."' (Schlemmer, *Briefe und Tagebücher,* p. 163.) There is, in fact, a strong affinity between Runge's disciplined style and the controlled style which Schlemmer adopted. He made a study of both Goethe's and Runge's theories of colour. As a dancer, he adopted the pseudonym Walter Schoppe (from a character in Jean Paul's *Titan*), and he was particularly fond of E. T. A. Hoffmann with his puppets, his automatons, and the inventive Dr. Spalanzani.

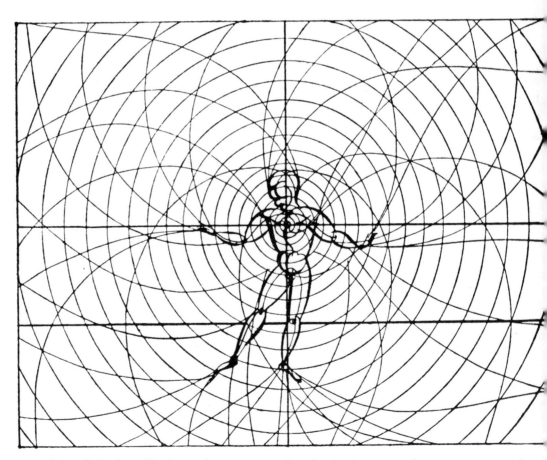

Oskar Schlemmer: The laws of organic man place him in the centre of an imaginary spatial relationship resulting from man's movements and his radial emanations. (From **Mensch und Kunstfigur,** in **Die Bühne am Bauhaus,** p. 14.)

The Bauhaus tenet 'Man is the measure of all things' owes much to Schlemmer, who placed man at the centre of his work. This applies also to Kandinsky who, contrary to a widely held belief, never lost sight of the human being, even in his abstract paintings. On the contrary, he based his aesthetics on a structure of perception inherent in human nature. Schlemmer, on the other hand, thought of man expressly in the context of the human body in relation to surrounding space. In its corporeality, it is clearly distinguished from the hollowness of the stereometric environment.

Schlemmer's significance for the Bauhaus was formulated by Georg Muche in the following words:

> He obviously knew—something we had all forgotten—that of all the visible shapes in nature, there is no such thing as the cube. We at the Bauhaus had placed ourselves under the sign of the right angle. The square was our favourite basic form. We sought the mysteries of creation in the hidden, invisible side of nature, and met a crystal-clear order, or the boundlessness of our own imagination. Oskar Schlemmer placed himself under the sign of the arc, the curve, and the circle. From these he formed the image of man, poised in harmonious movement. (Muche, *Blickpunkt*, p. 132.)

Oskar Schlemmer was born in Stuttgart on September 4, 1888. He inherited his love for the theatre from his father, Carl Theodor Schlemmer, a businessman who used to write plays which he produced in the amateur dramatic society of his businessman's club. When his parents died in 1900, Oskar went to live with his elder sister at Göppingen, where he attended secondary school. After serving a two-year apprenticeship in a local marquetry workshop, he was admitted in 1905 to the Stuttgart School of Arts and Crafts, and in 1909 received a grant to study at the Stuttgart Academy of Art. His individual development was greatly benefited by the teaching there, particularly that of Adolf Hölzel, whose master-class he joined in 1912. He formed a close friendship with Otto Meyer-Amden, and worked with Baumeister and Itten.

Toward Hölzel, he says he felt 'admiration because of his humanity, mixed with defiance, and even rejection of his teaching, with the result that there developed the best thing one could expect in the circumstances—a personal relationship'. (Schlemmer, *'Analyse eines Bildes und andere Dinge'* [Analysis of a Picture and Other Things], *Bauhaus*, Vol. III, No. 4, 1923.) For his fellow student Itten, he evinced a guarded interest which failed to deepen into anything more than a cool friendliness during their years together at the Bauhaus. On the other hand, he worked very closely with Baumeister, and for a short period this resulted in a striking stylistic similarity in their artistic experiments. They also exhibited jointly on several occasions. But Schlemmer's real teacher, though only a little older than himself, was Otto Meyer-Amden, whose limited but significant work deserves more notice. Here, in a nutshell, we find all the problems on which Schlemmer laboured throughout his vast output. It is therefore very understandable that Schlemmer felt the most profound esteem for his friend.

Schlemmer spent the years 1910—11 in Berlin and returned to the Stuttgart Academy of Art the following year. From 1914 to 1918, he served in the army. On his return from the war, he was elected to the Council of the Students' Union at the Stuttgart Academy, which he did not leave until 1920. He moved to Cannstadt in order to devote himself intensively to work on his ballet, and it was there that Gropius' offer of a teaching post reached him.

During his period at the Bauhaus, Schlemmer was engaged in oil and mural painting, sculpture, ballet, and the theatre. In both form and colour, the firm and rigorous style of his sober paintings was determined by his Apollonian attitude of mind which kept his artistic development directed toward a definite goal. Most of his colours were graded in muted scales of browns and greys. Only a few of his pictures contain predominating combinations of glowing red and strong blue. The contours of figures are simplified, and his formal language is one of restraint and of a calm serenity of expression. The same kind of pictorial concentration can be found in Seurat and Cézanne. A rigid stereometric line-ation of spatial persepective contrasts with the flow of tensioned curves, reminiscent of the waisted shapes of violins, cellos, guitars, and other stringed instruments.

Schlemmer's first outstanding paintings date from 1911–12 and include the studies of the *Jagdschloss Grunewald* (Hunting Lodge in the Grunewald, Hilde-brandt texts Nos. 3, 11), which, in their expansive Cubism, call to mind Braque's *L'Estaque pictures*. The effects on Schlemmer's style of his collaboration with Baumeister are most noticeable in the period between 1915–19, when he estab-lished his formal canon. The pictures of those years do not attempt to give an illusion of space; the compositions are flat and linear, and his symbols appear hieroglyphic. His only totally abstract painting, *Bild K* (Picture K, Hildebrandt, No. 13), was composed in 1915, and Schlemmer realized immediately that this was not his line. His painting reached its zenith during his years at the Bauhaus.

For the time being, as 'Master of Form' in charge of the stone-sculpture workshop, he devoted himself to problems of plastic form. He himself did very few sculptures, but his background as a painter led him to try his hand at reliefs. In cautious experiments to embed the human form in a supporting wall, he resorted to an austere combination of cup shapes, concave, convex, offset, and sometimes abruptly broken. The positives of these shapes corresponded in volume and rhythm with their negatives. Only two sculptures in the round are known: an *Abstrakte Figur* (Abstract Figure, Hildebrandt, No. 8), of 1921, exe-cuted in plaster and cast in bronze, which is in Mrs. Tut Schlemmer's collection, consists of interlocking capsules. The other sculpture, which is in wood, belongs to the Berlin National Gallery. Both figures stand on long, large feet, shaped peculiarly, like upturned boats pointed at one end, and acting as counterweights. To discover the nature of Schlemmer's work in this field, one has to turn to the experiments in sculpture made by his students.

In 1920, when he devoted most of his energy to ballet and other matters, Schlemmer painted only 2 water-colours, and no canvases at all. In 1921, he completed 3 pictures, 2 of which cannot be traced. Of the 2 pictures painted in 1922, *Tänzerin—die Geste* (Dancer—the Gesture, Hildebrandt, No. 20) is one of his major works. In 1923, he became more productive, completing 7 pictures, including one which shows, for the first time, a group in spatial relationship: *Tischgesellschaft* (Company at Table, Hildebrandt, No. 19). As far as is known, he did only 4 paintings in 1924 and 8 in 1925. The arrangement of figures into groups becomes more frequent, culminating in *Konzentrische Gruppe* (Concentric Group, Hildebrandt, No. 21). No canvases are known from the years 1926–27, and only a few water-colours. However, in 1928, he produced 28 paintings, and the same number again in 1929—his last year at the Bauhaus. In 1932, he painted in retrospect the well-known *Bauhaustreppe* (Staircase at the Bauhaus, Hildebrandt, No. 47).

Compared with his pre-1919 output, the paintings which Schlemmer produced at the Bauhaus belong to a maturer and more advanced phase. Perhaps stimulated by his stage activities, he introduced into his pictures a new dimension— the depth of space—which he had previously avoided. At this point, Schlemmer's major theme came into its own—the human being in space. Although his human figures have a fully rounded, corporeal appearance, and despite the fact that the rooms are always drawn in depth-creating perspective, this combination, though seemingly palpable, is neither realistic nor illusionist, but meant metaphysically. The figures represent man's counterpart, and the 'reality' depicted is always imaginary and sometimes unreal, because the human beings are depersonalized, their masklike faces are rigid and do not betray any feelings. The voluminous bodies–usually modelled in a well-rounded style, though occasionally flat–are reduced to their basic forms: cones, spheres, cylinders, and a peculiar pear shape which may have its origins in a hyperbola or, more probably, in a rotating body. The perspective, which looks convincing at first glance, turns out to contradict optical laws. It is an exaggerated perspective, irregular and mystifying as a result of numerous intersections. Light is given significance as magic luminosity, and its entry from a verifiable source cannot be ascertained. These human figures sit, stand, and walk in a kind of ritual gymnastics, in a house which consists of movable parts and screens. There is a feeling of an unseen labyrinth of rooms beyond. Because of their very palpability and heightened realism, the events in the picture are removed from the spectator's grasp, and we might well be gazing into Apollo's mirror as it reveals the mathematical precision of an ennobled transcendental existence freed from passion. In these pictures, stairs and banisters frequently recur as settings. Doors in rear walls open onto terraces from which, however, we are barred by the interior layout of the room: the middle distance is felt as a hermetic barrier. On the floors tiled in chess-board pattern, puppet-like figures move about mechanically, manipulated by some force which lies outside the visible sector of the picture—a situation which reminds us of the chess game in *Alice in Wonderland*.

Schlemmer's endeavours to revitalize the art of the dance are reflected in one of his first important paintings produced at the Bauhaus—the large picture *Tänzerin—die Geste* (Hildebrandt, No. 20), dated 1922–23. The dancer (a figurine from one of his ballets) is an expansive figure advancing dramatically toward the spectator in over-emphasized perspective. The swinging movement is abruptly frozen into a gesture. The upper body is vaulted. The supporting leg, grossly foreshortened, appears quite small, far at the rear, while the other leg is thrust forward, grotesquely enlarged. Though apparently stiff, its conical form could be the result of constant, fast rotation around an axis—motion solidified. The right arm repeats the thrusting movement of the leg, with the hand spread open in a gesture of negation. It serves to put the dancer at a distance from the world of the spectator. The pictorial space underlines the movement; a curving shell surrounding the figure forms a hollow alcove which cradles the body. The explosive force of the gesture establishes the composition on the diagonal. Depth is exaggerated by the perspective of the lines on the floor.

Tischgesellschaft (Hildebrandt, No. 19), of 1923, is one of the first of Schlemmer's paintings to employ a spatial arrangement of a group of people. The scene feels haunted and charged with menacing tension. In this painting also, internal depth is created, this time by means of a purely stereometric object—a bare table-top—with a vase strategically placed on it so as to accentuate the tension. In the foreground, her back turned on the spectator, a woman occupies the central axis of the picture. A copy-book lies open before her, but the perspective of its edges clashes with that of the table. A child sits on her left, at the long side of the table. At the other end of the table, the materialization of a menacing paternal being holds the two persons in the foreground under his spell. His dark core is surrounded by fluorescent contours which radiate a shimmering light of their own. Behind the wall on the left-hand side, one sees a transcendental male figure, for whom the wall is apparently permeable. The stranger has raised his hands in a gesture which sets up a triangular relationship between the adult figures. The child is enclosed in the equilateral triangle formed by the invisible lines of tension.

In such later works as *Römisches* (Roman, Hildebrandt, No. 32), of 1925, and *Fünf Männer im Raum* (Five Men in Space, Hildebrandt, No. 30), of 1928, the feeling of menace has completely disappeared, but an impression of distance remains, frequently created by the back view of the person in the immediate foreground. An oppressive stillness pervades these scenes. The static figures, arranged in meaningful relationships, whether turned toward or away from each other, seem to be awaiting the next move of a chess game directed from above, in which they are the pawns and pieces, crowded together on a small board.

Schlemmer designed his first mural in 1909–10 in collaboration with Meyer-Amden. In 1923, the main foyer of the Bauhaus—the former Art Academy of the Grand Duchy of Weimar, designed by Henry van de Velde—was remodelled to express the Bauhaus spirit. The stucco reliefs for the entrance hall were by Joost Schmidt; Oskar Schlemmer decorated it with murals. In connection with his plans for these, he wrote in his diary in November, 1922:

> The mural, with its distinctive relationship to space and architecture, must find a home and a solution at the Bauhaus. Free from the dangers of *l'art pour l'art* (Art for art's sake) and from the self-sufficiency of easel painting, the mural must have an ethical foundation; the ideas it depicts must have universal value, or at least embody values which will enable it to become universal. The purpose of the mural is the representation of epic themes. It still has its place today—today more than ever. The will to create it still lives, particularly in German art. (Schlemmer, *Briefe und Tagebücher*, pp. 137 ff.)

Now that he had real space to work on, Schlemmer no longer placed his human figures in three-dimensional perspective, as he had done in his paintings, but solved the problem of large-scale surfaces with flat, linear representation and with relief. On the semicircle of the wall above the staircase, shadowy figures floated in an ethereal dance. Above the doors on the ground floor were drawn linear figures of monumental proportions. Above the entrance door, the significance of a kneeling male nude was indicated by circles marking his head and chest to symbolize the forces of reason and of the soul. At the bottom of the stairs, metal-toned heroic relief figures stood guard over the upper floor.

After the Weimar Bauhaus was closed, the Art Academy was directed first by Otto Bartning and later by Paul Schultze-Naumburg, who became one of the cultural protagonists of Nazism in Thuringia. He possessed limited critical faculties and believed himself fully justified in having Schlemmer's mural destroyed in 1930.

Schlemmer made his first experiments with the dance in 1912. In a diary entry of December, 1912, he set down his ideas on the 'evolution of the dance from old to new', and, on January 5, 1913, he wrote to Otto Meyer-Amden that his reflections had been prompted by a performance of Arnold Schönberg's music. On the occasion of a charity concert given by his regiment in December, 1916, parts of his ballet were performed, which enabled him to awaken interest in his work and to establish some useful contacts. On February 11, he wrote to Meyer-Amden: 'Indeed, I can see great possibilities ahead for ballet and mime, because they are not dependent on historic subjects, as are drama and opera. This is why I believe that decisive innovations will come from this more limited but sensitive sphere of the stage.' (Schlemmer, *Briefe und Tagebücher*, p. 59.)

From 1919 onward, Schlemmer worked intensively on the realization of this ideas connected with the dance. In 1920, he made the acquaintance of Paul Hindemith, who wanted to write ballet music for him; Schlemmer was in the middle of this work when he was called to the Bauhaus. He took over the Bauhaus Theatre in 1923. Compared with Schreyer's emotive-calligraphic formulae, Schlemmer's designs and instructions are of great scientific precision and complexity.

Heinrich von Kleist's essay *Über das Marionettentheater* (On the Marionette Theatre) was frequently discussed by members of the Bauhaus Theatre, and this curious piece of German prose contains the key to a fundamental understanding of Schlemmer's ideas. Kleist, who had written the essay in dialogue form, had come to the conclusion that the divine harmony of creation—which is manifested in the graceful movements of innocence and in its sureness of instinct—was lost to man in his fall from grace. This is why man must remain imperfect in movement, even as a dancer. The puppet, on the other hand, which does not feel and which is controlled from outside—as if by a higher destiny—possesses the capacity for harmonious movement and therefore embodies the perfection of creation on a different plane—that of art. 'Once consciousness has passed as if through the infinite, grace returns; so that it appears in its purest form in that human body-form which has either infinite consciousness or none at all—in the puppet, or in the god.'

This sounds as if it were a commentary on Schlemmer's pictures. It expresses Schlemmer's ideas perfectly. Writing about his Triadic Ballet, Schlemmer noted in his diary on July 5, 1926:

> And why a mechanical organ? Because a mechanical instrument is exactly right for the stereotyped dance style which is partly the result of the body-mechanical mathematical costumes, and partly represents a deliberate departure from the prevalent dramatic emotional style. Moreover, a mechanical organ, with its music-box-like quality, will provide the perfect accompaniment to a stylized dance, and all these elements together should blend into a unity of style. Now one might say, why should not the dancers actually be marionettes, controlled by wires, or better still, by a device of perfect mechanical precision which would work automatically, almost without human interference except through an invisible control panel? Yes! It is only a question of time and money before the experiment can be perfected in this way. In *Über das Marionettentheater*, Heinrich von Kleist described the effect this would produce. (Schlemmer, *Briefe und Tagebücher*, p. 203.)

Thus, Schlemmer's ideas were evolving toward the puppet theatre. Schlemmer has often been accused of being a protagonist of a soulless mechanization, but this is a complete misunderstanding of his intentions. His object was precisely the opposite—to reconstruct God in man through the puppet-creature. The tragedy of dramatic art lies in the fact that in the last resort this is impos-

Oskar Schlemmer: The laws of cubic space determine the invisible network of lines consisting of planimetric and stereometric relations. (From **Mensch und Kunstfigur, in Die Bühne am Bauhaus,** p. 13.)

sible, because imperfection is inherent in the human condition. 'Not the machine —not abstraction—always the human being.' (Schlemmer, *Briefe und Tagebücher*, p. 122.)

Schlemmer published a number of articles in which he expounded his ideas on the dance, drama, and ballet. In these, he formulated a theoretical foundation of his art which is relevant not only to his stage experiments but also to his paintings, where he merely transposed the choreography of his ballets onto an imaginative plane. His reflections were summed up in Volume IV of the Bauhaus Books, which was brought out in 1925 and devoted to the Bauhaus Theatre, in an essay entitled 'Mensch und Kunstfigur' (Man and 'Art Figure' or 'Artificial Figure'). The title is revealing, since the word *Kunstfigur* establishes a connection with German Romanticism. It evokes not only the mechanical perfection of Kleist's marionettes, but also the talking Turk in *The Automaton*, (one of the *Tales* of E. T. A. Hoffmann) and the character of Olympia in Hoffmann's story *The Sandman*. The word probably appears for the first time in Clemens Brentano's *Fairy-tale of Gockel and Hinkel*, with its refrain: *'Keine Puppe, es ist nur eine schöne Kunstfigur'* (It's not a puppet—just a beautiful *Kunstfigur*).

Schlemmer conducted an intensive investigation into the 'experience of space', to discover the basic laws which govern 'man as a dancer' and which determine measurable relations between the human form and space. Schlemmer found two fundamental relationships. The first consists of the planimetric

27. Schlemmer, Three Profiles, 1922—tempera on paper

28. Schlemmer, Concentric Group, 1925—oil on canvas

29. Schlemmer, Company at Table, 1923—oil on canvas

30. Schlemmer, Abstract Figure—Sculpture in the round, 1921—nickeled bronze

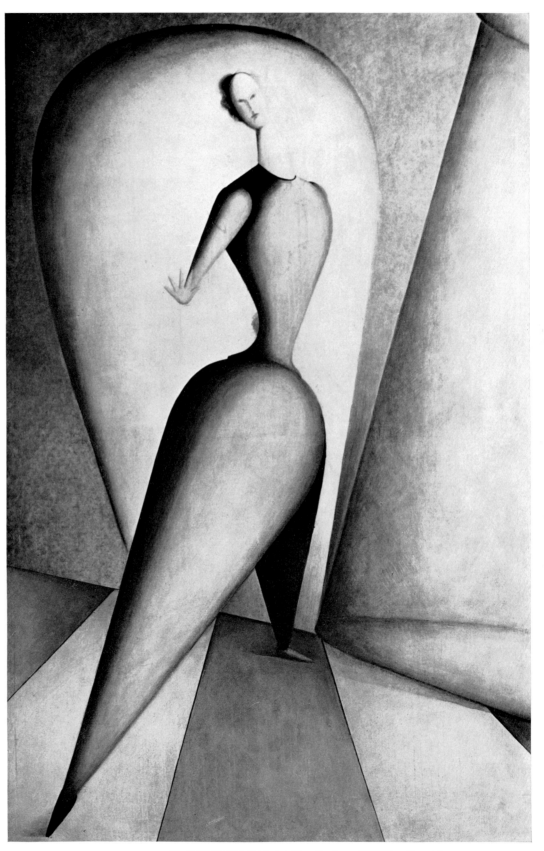

31. Schlemmer, Dancer—The Gesture, 1922/23—oil and tempera on canvas

32. Schlemmer, Man Passing by, 1924—oil on canvas

33. Schlemmer, Roman, 1925—oil on canvas

34. Schlemmer, Between Columns, 1928—water-colour

35. Schlemmer, Group of Light-coloured Figures, 1936—pencil an chalk

36. Schlemmer, Staircase at the Bauhaus, 1932—water-colour

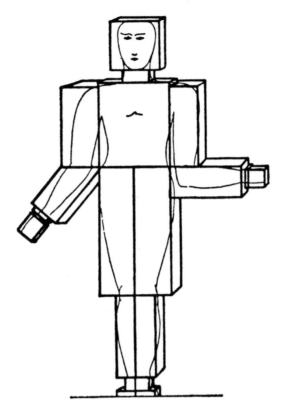
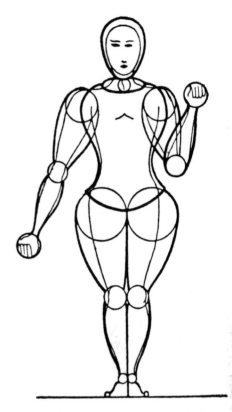
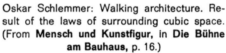

Oskar Schlemmer: Walking architecture. Result of the laws of surrounding cubic space. (From **Mensch und Kunstfigur,** in **Die Bühne am Bauhaus,** p. 16.)

Oskar Schlemmer: The 'jointed puppet'. Result of the functional laws of the human body in relation to space. (From **Mensch und Kunstfigur,** in **Die Bühne am Bauhaus,** p. 16.)

and stereometric relationship to cubic space, which is the result of our own innate consciousness of co-ordinates. External space—apart from gravitation—is neutral, but we perceive its dimensions indirectly, and we therefore shape our rooms as cubes. The person who stands up in front of others to make them believe something, at first creates an invisible stage around himself, which eventually assumes real shape in the 'stage box' of the theatre. The stereometric relationship holds us in space as in a glass cage. The other relationship is the opposite of the first. It is caused by the natural rotations of our organic movements, which fill space with a vibrating net of radial emanations. The dancer is a person who, with his movements, tries to overcome the force of gravity; but this can never be accomplished in perfection. As Schlemmer said:

> The striving to release man from his limitations and to increase his freedom of movement beyond its natural range leads to the replacement of the human organism by the mechanical *Kunstfigur:* automaton and puppet. The *Kunstfigur* makes possible any movement, any position, in any time interval whatsoever, and it permits a device used by great artists in their heyday: a variation in the size relationship between the figures, so that important characters are large, unimportant ones small. Another

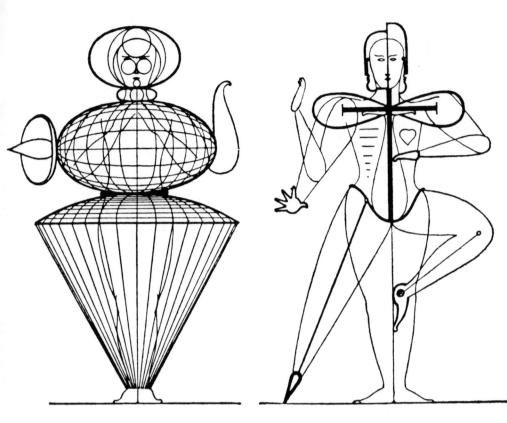

Oskar Schlemmer: A technical organism. Result of the laws of motion of the human body in space. (From **Mensch und Kunstfigur,** in **Die Bühne am Bauhaus,** p. 17.)

Oskar Schlemmer: Dematerialization. Result of metaphysical forms of expression. (From **Mensch und Kunstfigur,** in **Die Bühne am Bauhaus,** p. 17.)

significant result is the possibility of establishing a relationship between the naturally naked human being and the abstract figure, both of which are enhanced in their essential nature.

Here, Schlemmer got to the heart of the problem and, at the same time, found a justification for the abstract mask costumes which he designed, and which his brother Carl executed in accordance with his precise instructions. These costumes were developed from the conception of movement in space. In his essay, Schlemmer described the basic types: The laws of cubic space permit the creation of a figure from rectangles, 'walking architecture.' The laws of human body movement result in the creation of a rotational figure, a 'technical organism'. Several variants of such figures appeared in the Triadic Ballet, as well as a 'jointed puppet' derived from the functional laws of the human body, which represents the real archetype of the Schlemmerian figure. As a mask, this figure is found in the Triadic Ballet, swinging a club. The symbolism of the human body structure leads to a 'metaphysical form of expression': the star, the cross, the Janus head, and figurations which belong to several categories at the same time.

The Triadic Ballet, first performed at the Stuttgart State Theatre in 1922, expresses in dance the interrelationships of the Trinity. It was constructed with mathematical precision, as Schlemmer had an almost cabbalistic obsession with the numerical symbolism of mathematical relationships. All the dances which were later performed at the Bauhaus derive from the Triadic Ballet. There followed, in 1922–23, *Das figurale Kabinett* (Cabinet of Figures); in 1924, *Meta oder die Pantomime der Örter* (Meta, or the Mime of Places); in 1925, the mime *Treppenwitz* (Afterthought); and many others. Schlemmer tried to give shape to his fundamental ideas in pure form in the 1927 productions of *Raumtanz* (Dance of Space), *Stäbetanz* (Dance of Staves), and *Reifentanz* (Dance of Hoops). In contrast to Schreyer, who neglected this· important dramatic element, Schlemmer did not avoid the comic and the grotesque—on the contrary, he emphasized it, even to the extent of clowning.

When Hannes Meyer took over the direction of the Bauhaus, he saw no need for a Bauhaus Theatre. Schlemmer therefore accepted an offer to teach at the State Academy of Art, Breslau. He left Dessau in October, 1929. On April 1, 1932, the Breslau Academy was closed down by an emergency regulation. Schlemmer felt helpless in the face of the brutality of Nazism. Having been officially declared 'decadent', he could not take in what was going on, and, for a long time, a deep melancholia prevented him from doing any artistic work. In the late 1930's, he worked for a house-painter in Stuttgart. In 1940, Kurt Herberts asked him to join his paint laboratory at Wuppertal, and in that town, Schlemmer found Baumeister, Marcks, and Muche. In 1942, he painted the small window-pictures, which were his last works. He died in Baden-Baden on April 13, 1943. Schlemmer, the fashioner of men, had maintained an inner distance from the men around him. Tragedy had cast its shadow over both his life and his work.

PAUL KLEE

On November 25, 1920, Paul Klee and his family were staying with Alexei Jawlensky and Marianne von Werefkin, when the following telegram arrived: 'Dear Paul Klee. We unanimously beg you to honour us by coming as a painter to the Bauhaus. Gropius, Feininger, Engelmann, Marcks, Muche, Itten, Klemm.' The previous year, the students of the Stuttgart Academy, led by Oskar Schlemmer, had tried to get Klee appointed as one of their teachers. However, the Stuttgart professors opposed this move, and it came to nothing. When Klee received the call to the Bauhaus, he accepted it without hesitation. In December, he made an exploratory trip to Weimar. When Schlemmer met him at the station, the first thing Klee asked was a number of searching questions about food prices. Though this may not fit in with the common idea of the unworldliness of artists, it does at least show that Klee exercized the same economy of means in his personal affairs as in his art.

He moved to Weimar in January, 1921, leaving his family to follow him in September of that year. He was short in stature, refined, well-dressed, and of a reserved disposition. He had dark, piercing eyes and features which have been described as Moorish. He used to wear a hard hat, fashionable at the time, oddly perched above his high, handsome forehead, which made his head seem out of proportion to the rest of his body. When teaching, he often dressed casually and smoked a pipe in the studio. His observations were kindly, though laced with a gentle sarcasm. An aura of benevolent wisdom surrounded him, earning him the respectful nickname of 'Der liebe Gott' ('Our Father in Heaven').

Klee was originally appointed to take charge of the bookbinding workshop, and from 1922 he also directed the glass-painting workshop, but both appointments were purely nominal. During his whole time at the Bauhaus, he was seen only a few times in the bookbinding workshop. His major achievement was the theory of form which he developed and taught in the advanced course that followed on from Itten's basic course. Klee's lessons were difficult. In collected form, they constitute a penetrating and fundamental contribution to twentieth-century art theory, aptly complemented by the observations made by Kandinsky in his lectures. The twin stars Klee and Kandinsky were the crowning constellation in the Bauhaus firmament. Their artistic dialogue went far beyond the bounds of mere speculation, and their exact investigations led to discoveries of scientific value, opening up new vistas in art. Klee and Kandinsky had known each other for years. They had studied together under the same teachers, and had been close friends since their Blaue Reiter days at Munich. Later, at Dessau, they lived next to each other in the masters' houses.

Of all the artists who taught at the Bauhaus, Paul Klee, with his spiritual universality, is the most difficult to assess. Johannes Itten had the markings of a demagogue; Wassily Kandinsky was a dogmatist; Klee was far removed from either of these extremes. In his teaching, he was reluctant to give a definite opinion, and when he did make an unqualified statement, he was liable to retract it in the next sentence, afraid it might be taken for gospel truth.

Klee was very fond of the writings of Novalis, the early nineteenth-century Romantic, with whom he had a great deal in common. Both had a consistent philosophy of life which, however, they were careful not to turn into a 'system'. Both expressed themselves poetically or in crisp aphorisms that illuminated a problem in a flash, without robbing it of its mystery or presenting it as a cut-and-dried solution. Klee wrote in his diary:

> In this world, I am not really comprehensible. I dwell both with the dead and with the unborn. A little closer to the heart of creation than most people. And yet not close enough. Do I radiate warmth? Coolness? This is irrelevant—I am beyond all passion. When I am furthest away, I am most pious. In this world, perhaps a little uncharitable. But this is only a trifle. The clerics are not pious enough to see it that way. And any trifle is enough to annoy these scribes.

Indeed, he is not comprehensible in this world. But if not here, where, and how? Is he an eccentric, an alchemist, or an Oriental wizard with a genie at his command? Somehow this extravagant language seems inappropriate for Paul Klee—none of his works is done on a large scale; some, in fact, are miniatures, and all are intended to be seen from close quarters. What mattered to him was not the coverage of monumental space with broad gestures, but a concise formulation of emotion, monumentality, and gesture compressed into the smallest possible space. He endeavoured to find a valid formula for each particular problem, and for this, a few square centimetres were enough. Every single work of Klee's is a perfect example, but an example of what? According to Will Grohmann, three groups can be clearly distinguished in his work at the Bauhaus: an outer, a middle, and an inner circle (Grohmann, *Paul Klee*, pp. 189 ff.). In the works of the outer circle, Klee concerns himself with phenomena of life and nature as they are presented to our senses through the environment. In the middle circle, he penetrates the depths of symbolic pictorial laws which allow full scope to the imagination. The inner circle comprises those pictures which formulate the mystery of an insoluble existential equation, infinite in itself, with such penetration and precision that any additional interpretation would not add to its understanding. Therefore, the pictures of the inner circle are of the greatest import, as they convey an impression of absolute finality which Klee achieved by travelling along a hallucinatory path to the border where the dividing wall between existence and transcendence is but wafer-thin. On this transparent plane of projection, the fundamental realities of life and cognition can only just be perceived as insubstantial coloured shadows. The mirror of consciousness no longer throws back a reflection; it has become a window. In these pictures, the approximation of a transcendental zero point has been reached.

Hallucination does not imply a state of trance, but rather clarity of vision. Klee often designed his pictures with the preciseness of a scientist, adding a touch here and a touch there with mathematical exactitude. But suddenly—like a secret ingredient added by a master-chef—Klee's final touch transforms the picture and brings about a perfection which lifts it out of the realm of rational explanation.

The artistic philosophy of all the painters whom we have discussed so far, had a common metaphysical orientation, which, as we shall see, was shared also by Kandinsky. The attempt to penetrate the mysteries which lie beyond our cognition led the most important streams of twentieth-century art to move away from mere representation of the visible world or to abandon it altogether. Klee's ideas, too, were rooted in metaphysics. In a lecture on colour, he said, on November 28, 1922:

> However, the imperfection of appearance can be partly overcome with the aid of our creative ability which should enable us to attain at least a synthesis of the perfection of transcendental existence. We assume that what reaches us as imperfect appearance, does exist somewhere without imperfections, and our artistic instincts must help us to reconstruct the form of that existence. (Klee, *Das bildnerische Denken* [Pictorial Thinking], p. 467.)

Nevertheless, among all these metaphysicians, Klee is somehow different. He does not quite fit in. While the others are fascinated by the reproduction of a personal mental image of a possible transcendental reality, Klee is interested in the functioning of the transcendental process itself, which he investigates with the engrossed curiosity of a researcher, trying to take it apart like an engine, perhaps hoping to be able to ferret out by close analysis the mechanics behind it.

He usually worked on several pictures at the same time. He would sit in his studio, contemplating the works in progress, and wait until he was inspired to add something here or something there. One might say that after bringing his work to a certain stage of completion, he lay in wait to see what would fall into his trap; he would wait until the spirit emerged, as it were, through the back of the picture on to its surface. Then the picture was really complete, and Klee would say: 'Now it is looking at me.' He thought of himself as a customs official guarding the border traffic between this world and the beyond.

This kind of creative attitude can be explained by Klee's particular way of looking at things, in terms of their 'physiognomy'. It must be remembered that physiognomy is formed by the encounter of inner processes—mental and intellectual—with the outside world. The physiognomist is able to draw conclusions as to the invisible events which hide behind the exterior surface, by examining the zone of encounter between the internal and the external, as on a pictorial surface. This is how Klee's famous opening sentence to his 'creative confession' of 1920 must be understood: 'Kunst gibt nicht das Sichtbare wieder, sondern macht sichtbar' (Art does not render the visible; it renders visible').

Picture titles containing this word frequently occur in his work: *Physiognomy of a Plantation—Physiognomy of Gloom—Physiognomical Crystallization—Physiognomy in the Manner of a Small Portrait—Mystical-Physiognomical—Physiognomy of a Dream—Physiognomy of a Landscape.* Even his early etchings of 1903–5 are basically physiognomical allegories, in particular: *Drohendes Haupt, Perseus* (Menacing Head, Perseus); *Der Witz hat über das Leid gesiegt* (Wit has conquered Sorrow); and *Komiker* (Comic); *Die Jungfrau im Baum* (The Virgin in the Tree); and *Der Held mit dem Flügel* (The Hero with the Wing).

Over the years, Klee produced a number of self-portraits with a masklike character which he explained in physiognomical terms:

> Many people will not recognize the truthfulness of my mirror. They should remember that my purpose is not to mirror the surface (the photographic plate can do that) but to penetrate the interior. I mirror right into the heart. I write the words on the forehead and around the corners of the mouth. My human faces are more truthful than the real ones. If I were to paint a completely true self-portrait, one would see a strange crust. And one would have to explain that I am inside, like the kernel in a nut. One might also call this work an 'Allegory of Encrustation'. (Klee, *Das bildnerische Denken*, p. 8.)

Klee called a self-portrait of 1922 *Gespenst eines Genies* (Spectre of a Genius). Its core is formed by a balanced structure composed of a chain of hanging trapezes. The precisely constructed scaffolding consists of transverse beams, hanging ropes, and interlocking wheels. A finely balanced pendulum movement can be imagined which allows the whole internal structure to swing backwards and forwards on the lower beam of the trapeze. Klee surrounds this airy skeleton with the shell of the external figure, producing an ironic anatomy.

For Klee, the word 'physiognomy' meant, not only the reflection of human characteristics in facial expression, but a general principle. It is possible to follow the various stages of his development in this direction. Script and its characters have a physiognomic meaning. Klee was left-handed and, like Leonardo da Vinci, was ambidextrous and able to do mirror-writing. He divested script of the administrative character deriving from its literary associations, thus discovering its own semantic value. This was a continuation of the tradition which had its precursors in Caballistic texts and the calligraphy of the Baroque. Klee playfully designed an abstract script, the liberated characters of which have a magical effect, as if embodying messages from unknown spheres. In this connection, there is a strong artistic relationship with Willi Baumeister, who expressed similar ideas in *Das Unbekannte in der Kunst* (The Unknown in Art).

Physiognomy as a cosmic doctrine is not a new idea first formulated by Klee, but represents a specialized branch of European cultural history. Carl Gustav Carus wrote about a *Cosmic Symbolism and Physiognomy,* and similar lines of thought can be found in the writings of Goethe, Novalis, Runge, and Tieck, who are representative of the Romantic movement. But Klee's picture titles, such as *Physiognomie des Traumes* (Physiognomy of a Dream) and *Landschaftlichen Physiognomie* (Physiognomy of a Landscape), lead us even further back in history. Isa Lohmann-Siehms has recently pointed out a relationship between twentieth-century art theories and the physiognomy of the eighteenth century, expressed by J. C. A. Grohmann and Anton Joseph Pernety (*Jahrbuch der Hamburger Kunstsammlungen* [Yearbook of the Hamburg Art Collection], Vol. VIII, 1963, pp. 67 ff.; Vol. IX, 1964, pp. 49 ff.). In 1784, Pernety described physiognomy as a general science, and postulated separate physiognomies of vegetable life, of past epochs, of the state, and of nature. He concluded: 'Everything bears on its exterior a distinguishing mark, a hieroglyphic image, from which the observer can easily make deductions about secret forces and qualities.' There is no more succinct explanation of Klee's art.

Isa Lohmann-Siems draws our attention to the fact that only a certain observant type of person can perceive the physiognomy of an object in this manner. Goethe called this quality 'intuitive reasoning power,' and Kant, *intellectus archetypus. (Jahrbuch der Hamburger Kunstsammlungen* I, Vol. IX, p. 58). Finally, the European origin of a doctrine of universal characters, which can also be understood pantheistically, is to be found in Neo-Platonism and in some branches of medieval philosophy. The belief that the universe is mirrored in its parts has led to the concept of the analogous pair: macrocosm-micro-

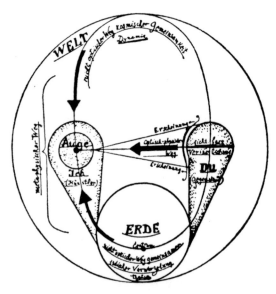

Paul Klee: Paths of nature study. Diagram illustrating the essay **Wege des Naturstudiums,** published in **Staatliches Bauhaus Weimar 1919–23.**

cosm. Thus, Paracelsus taught that a perfect representation of the macrocosm can be found in the microcosm. Fundamentally, Klee was of the same opinion, as can be seen from many of his writings, but most clearly from the ideographic sketch which he produced for his essay *Wege des Naturstudiums* (Paths of Nature Study) in 1923.

In the same essay, writing about artistic creation, Klee came to the following conclusion:

All paths meet in the eye, where they are converted into form, and produce a synthesis of external looking and internal seeing. Starting from this meeting-point, manually-made structures are formed which, though completely divergent from the optical impression of an object, are not inconsistent with its total reality. The student transforms his various experiences into work, by means of which he displays the degree he has reached in his dialogue with the natural object. His progress in the contemplation and study of nature, and towards a mature philosophy of life, gives him the power to produce free abstract forms, which achieve a new naturalness in his work, transcending any deliberately schematic forms. Thus he creates a work (or is involved in the creation of works) which are analogous to the works of God.

Paul Klee was born at Münchenbuchsee, near Berne, on December 18, 1879. Like Feininger, he came from a musical family. His German father, Hans Klee, taught music at a teacher-training college. His mother, Ida Klee, was Swiss. Paul Klee himself was a virtuoso violinist. His gift for music showed itself at an early age, and as an adolescent, he played in the Berne municipal orchestra. He had considered becoming a professional musician before finally deciding otherwise. In 1906, he married a distinguished pianist, Lily Stumpf, whom he had met in Munich. His school years in Berne provided him with a sound and broadly-based education, which was valuable for his later work and philosophical reflections. From 1898 to 1901, he studied in Munich at Erwin Knirr's school of art and at the Munich Academy of Art under Franz Stuck. This is where he met Kandinsky. In 1901–2 he travelled to Italy with his friend Hermann Haller, the sculptor. In 1906, he finally moved to Munich. In 1911, he made contact with the Blaue Reiter circle and became friendly with its members. In 1912, he met Robert Delaunay in Paris and familiarized himself with the problems of Cubism. In 1914, in company with Louis Moilliet and August Macke, he travelled to Tunis, Sidi-bou-Said, Carthage, and Kairouan. His experiences during this journey brought about a turning-point in his artistic development. From 1916 to 1918, Klee served in the German army. At the time of his Bauhaus appointment, he was forty-one.

From his earliest work, Klee's output was characterized by fantasy and humour. His earlier pictures, particularly etchings, were overloaded with ideas and owed their allegorical character to content rather than form. In 1905, he started painting on the back of glass-panes—a technique which he and Kandinsky probably borrowed from Bavarian folk-art.

In 1911, he did a series of drawings to illustrate Voltaire's *Candide*. Like other works of this period, these display an irritable style of short strokes, which gives an insight into Klee's character and temperament not so easily discernible through the mature artistic wisdom of his later style. At this time, Klee drew a number of ironic and fantastic figure compositions and also landscapes, including the central station at Munich. These drawings bear a marked resemblance to Alfred Kubin's works. They are not strictly allegories, nor are they parables. Many of these drawings look as if their restless lines had been drawn in mid-air. Earthly matter rising from the ground in the form of bundles of thread blown about by the wind, remains hanging in limbo. But by 1913, Klee

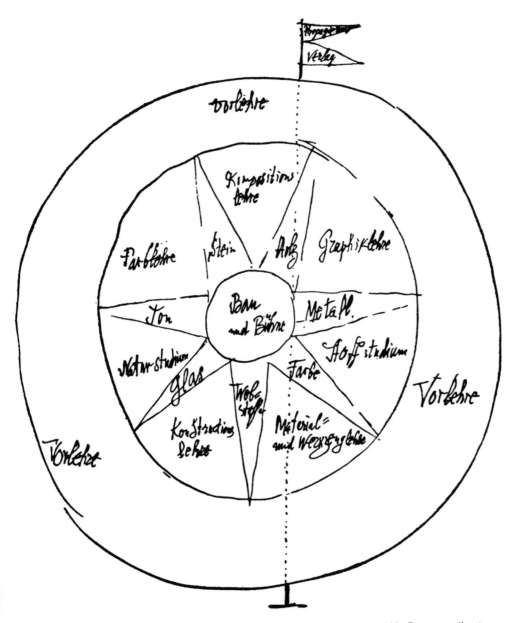

Paul Klee: Idea and structure of the Staatliches Bauhaus. Pen drawing, 1922. Private collection, Darmstadt. (From Wingler, **Das Bauhaus**, p. 11.)

was gradually moving away from this style, and his classic calligraphic style was beginning to emerge in pure form. The light touch evident in Klee's imaginative themes is reminiscent of the poetry of Christian Morgenstern, whose *Galgenlieder* he loved. A spiritual affinity with Klee is also discernible in Morgenstern's drawings. Both as a poet and as a painter, Morgenstern could be described as a 'gay' philosopher'. Both artists had a lot in common, particularly in the irony with which they treated their subjects. A characteristic instance is Klee's *Fliehende Polizisten* (Fleeing Policemen), of 1913 (Grohmann, *Paul Klee*, p. 55); they are pursued by the artist's mockery.

Klee's association with the artists of the Blaue Reiter and his study of Cubism had a great influence on him. He met Delaunay in Paris in 1912, but it was not until 1914 that Cubist elements became evident in Klee's style. It was in that year that he painted *Homage to Picasso* (Grohmann, *Paul Klee*, p. 131). Cubism brought Klee significant enrichments in the form, design, and composition of his works. During this period, he evolved the technique of constructing his pictures from coloured squares, which dominated his later work. During the 1920's, he developed this style into a system, freely paraphrasing the language of French Cubism until it became his own specific version of German Romanticism. At the same time, he made a careful study of Delaunay's theory of colour. Klee had been painting water-colours since 1911, but it was his journey to Tunis and Kairouan in 1914 that finally inspired him to work in colour. Refracted in a rainbow of colours, reality was represented in dream landscapes.

Klee had now reached a level where the work of art becomes a symbol of the seen world. One of the most beautiful examples of this is the water-colour *The Niesen* of 1915 (Grohmann, *Klee*, p. 126). That peak in the Bernese Oberland has been transformed by the artist's hand into a blue magic mountain with sun, moon, and stars. Following this, he painted what Grohmann has called his 'Cosmic Picture Book of 1916 to 1920'. These are truly jewels—poetic and lyrical metaphors of 'transcendental natural history', displaying Klee's own personal hieroglyphic script. Just before Klee joined the Bauhaus, he had perfected his style to full maturity. In 1919, he painted *Villa R*, which showed a conflict resolved. The letter 'R' as an abstract symbol has been noumenally absorbed into the formal destiny of the pictorial landscape.

Through his teaching at the Bauhaus, Klee was able to extend still further the diversity of pictorial means which he had at his command. Klee took his teaching most seriously, particularly as it served to expound his artistic philosophy. To help him in the preparation of his lectures, he bought a geometry textbook, and he used to jot down the subjects of his lectures in small blue notebooks.

Georg Muche describes one of his lectures as follows:

His lectures, which he prepared meticulously, always contained words of wisdom. For his first lesson at the Bauhaus, he entered the classroom with his back to the students, and without giving them so much as a glance, made straight for the blackboard, where he started talking and drawing. His spoken words were accompanied by chalked illustrations which he concluded by drawing two curving lines, touching at one end and intersecting at the other. Lo and behold, a fish! One curve starting on top of the tail fin, formed the line of the belly, rising up to end at the mouth. The other curve started at the lower point of the tail fin, arched over the back and met the first curve at the fish's mouth. Then Paul Klee said' "And this is Columbus' fish!", closed his book, and left the room (Muche, *Blickpunkt*, p. 140.)

In fact, Columbus' fish was invented by Klee not in his first lesson at the Bauhaus, but during a lecture on January 16, 1922 (Klee, *Das bildnerische Denken*, pp. 264 ff.; p. 297). His aim was to make clear to the students the difference between the dividual and the individual, the divisible series and the indivisible organism. The visible world is composed of building bricks which are identical at one stage and can be added together in regular series. The question is, how does one progress from one qualitative stage to the next higher stage? Klee made this clear by drawing rows of scales arranged like the tiles of a roof. The result was an aggregation but not an individual. 'The dividual is always the lower form', he said. But how does one reach the next higher individual from this point? Not by adding row upon row of identical forms to infinity, but by finding new, superior forms which represent a different entity. 'The individual is the higher form', and he illustrated his words by drawing the curves of the fish body around the scales. But when a number of fish are gathered together in one place, then they in turn become the dividual, and the next higher individual is the fish world united in an aquarium or pond.

In his teaching at the Bauhaus, Klee attempted to formulate the laws of nature—physical and mathematical—in relation to our perception of them. He did this in the form of functional analogies and allegories of pictorial formulae. Underlying his theories, there was a broad universality of ideas which he had shaped into a philosophic unity. Klee once expressed in tabular form the various possibilities of our formal perception in different fields. It conveyed his ideas about the *Gesamtkunstwerk*—the 'integral work of art'. He told his students: 'Of course, you do not have to learn this by heart. Each one of you will find something in this table that will make him feel at home.' (Klee, *Das bildnerische Denken*, p. 461.) In so far as a drawing is a functional formula of the laws of perception, the picture is the result of a movement which re-enacts the function. Klee began with the point; from the movement of the point, he developed the line; from the movement of the line, there emerged the plane. Explaining this process, he wrote:

Movement is the basis of all creation. In Lessing's *Laokoon*, on which we wasted a lot of thought and effort in our young days, much is made of the difference between art in time and space. But when examined closely, this turns out to be just scholarly nonsense. After all, space is one aspect of time. When a point becomes movement and therefore a line, it takes time. Similarly, when a line shifts to become a plane. Equally, the movement of planes to become volume. Has a picture ever been created instantaneously? No, it is built up piece by piece, as a house is built.

Thus, the picture is the result of a step-by-step movement which has come to rest, changing its function from an event in time into a simultaneous event in space. As the artist has travelled in his picture from point to point, so the eye follows the same course, and the spectator is able to retrace the path outlined by the artist. What Klee taught was his own artistic method. His pictures are the result of the wanderings of his pencil and his brush. In his essay 'Klee's Angels and Islands', Walter Ueberwasser showed the path followed by Klee's hand, for instance, in the drawing *Der wachsame Engel* (The Vigilant Angel), retracing his movements from the first to the twelfth stroke (Ueberwasser, *Festschrift Kurt Bauch* [Essays in Honour of Kurt Bauch], 1957, pp. 256 ff.).

To avoid purposeless wandering of the pencil, the important thing, however, is careful balancing of the drawing until the composition has come to rest. In Klee's work, an important rôle is played by scales and the concept of weighing. All of his work is carefully 'weighed', that is, balanced, and he taught that if a composition is overweight at one point, an equivalent must be 'added' at another point, and by adding something here and something there, the picture grows towards perfection. In his lessons, Klee dealt with form, structure, value, weight, line, plane, space, dimension, concentration, variation, perspective, rhythm, movement, statics, dynamics, tension, equilibrium, articulation, natural processes by which form is created, water, plants, gravity, light and dark, colour, and much more besides. His works provide many illustrations of his teachings. Nevertheless, his artistic work transcends his teaching by a final degree of intensity which is beyond description or explanation.

His life's work is so vast and many-sided that it is impossible to do it full justice within the framework of this book. However, we would point out a few themes of which he was particularly fond—namely, arrows, birds, fishes, phantoms, and angels. What unites these diverse beings is their mercurial character. They are all on the move towards a destination. Like Mercury, the God of traders and the postman who sped between Mount Olympus and mankind, they are messengers. The arrow is a messenger hastened to its target by the bowstring. There is no need to enlarge on the mercurial qualities of the arrow-fast bird. The arrow-shaped fish—Christian symbol—an alien-seeming being, lives in the mediate world of water, where man can see but not breathe, in a world which exists between our familiar surroundings of air and firm ground. The phantom is a messenger from an unknown sphere, and the angel is a messenger from heaven. 'The thought is the father of the arrow: how do I extend the limits of my realm?', Klee says in his *Pedagogical Sketchbook*. The essence of the human tragedy lies in the constrast between man's impotence on the physical plane and his power on the plane of ideas to extend his earthly and super-natural realms.

Klee's favourite instrument of demonstration is the arrow, which frequently appears in his works. Sometimes, it only serves as an imaginary direction sign, as in the painting *Abfahrt der Schiffe* (Departure of the Ships), of 1927 (Klee, *Das bildnerische Denken*, p. 80). In the picture *Arrow in the Garden*, of 1929 (Klee, *Das bildnerische Denken*, p. 56), it is a harbinger of destiny in a fragile landscape, while in *Betroffener Ort* (Stricken Place), of 1922 (Grohmann, *Paul Klee*, p. 393), it signifies grave forebodings. In the water-colour *Scheidung abends* (Evening Parting), of 1922 (Klee, *Das bildnerische Denken*, p. 11), the arrow recognizes itself, and in the drawing *Der Pfeil vor dem Ziel* (Arrow Approaching the Target, Grohmann, *Paul Klee*, p. 168), it has assumed the shape of an animal demon. Klee also uses stars with the same doom-laden con-notation as the arrow.

Of his fish pictures, one of the best-known is *Um den Fisch* (Around the Fish) in the Hamburg Kunsthalle collection. A mysterious companion picture of 1926 (Grohmann, *Paul Klee*, p. 229) shows a cosmic dance around the fish, which leads through the narrow passes of diverse forms of existence, polarized by the Christian cross and human understanding. Another example is *Fisch-zauber* (Fish Magic), of 1925 (Grohmann, *Paul Klee*, p. 211).

There are many representations of phantoms in Klee's work. Two charac-teristic examples are *Botschaft des Luftgeistes* (Message of the Air Spirit), of 1920 (Grohmann, p. 140), and *Materialisierte Gespenster* (Materialized Ghosts), of 1923 (San Lazzaro, *Paul Klee*, p. 76). In these drawings, seriousness is tinged with irony.

Angels appeared in many of Klee's works and became more frequent as his life and work neared their end. Finally, they sang his requiem and carried him away from his art. An angel appears as part of the still-life which was Klee's last picture (Grohmann, *Paul Klee*, p. 363).

In *Grenzen des Verstandes* (Frontiers of Reason), of 1927, Klee attempted to depict a transcendental process in cross-section. In a few works of the 'inner circle' described by Grohmann, called *Magische Quadrate* (Magic Squares) and *Streifen und Rasterbilder* (Stripes and Screens) (Grohmann, *Paul Klee*, p. 395), Klee resorted to a harmonious 'chromatic' treatment of the background, either to create an abstract pattern or to depict in playful and delicate outlines some representational object. Klee, the musician, tried to give a *Pictorial Representa-tion of a Musical Theme from a Movement in Three Voices by Johann Sebastian Bach* (Klee, *Das bildnerische Denken*, p. 286–87). Here, his painting came close to representing in pictorial form the laws of musical harmony. He tried to eavesdrop on Creation to discover its musical score. The text of his water-colour script of 1918 (Grohmann, *Paul Klee*, p. 153) describes the parabolic curve of his work in these words: 'Once arisen from the gray of night / then

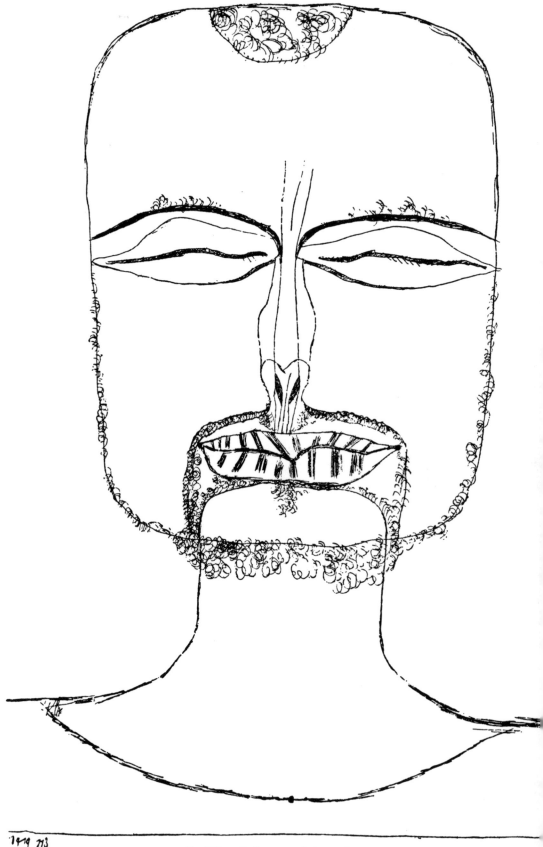

Paul Klee: Self-portrait. Lithograph, 1919.

heavy and dear / and strengthened by fire / now ethereally surrounded by blue / soars above eternal snows / towards sapient stars.'

Klee left the Bauhaus in 1931 and accepted a professorship at the Düsseldorf Art Academy. Vilified by the Nazis as 'decadent', he was dismissed in 1933. He returned to Switzerland and settled in Berne. During the last years of his life, Klee was very ill, suffering from sclerosis (the drying-up of the mucous membranes). He died at Muralto, near Locarno, on July 29, 1940. He had applied for Swiss citizenship, which was delayed by bureaucratic red tape and, when it finally came, arrived too late. Thus, Klee died a German against his wish. Klee's late work, dating from his post-Bauhaus period, has not yet found the public recognition it deserves.

37. Klee, Houses by the Sea, 1920/134—water-colour

38. Klee, Garden Architecture, 1919/158—oil on board

39. Klee, Villa R., 1919/153—tempera and oil

40. Klee, Spectre of a Genius, 1922/10—water colour

41. Klee, Red/Violet/Yellow-Green, Terraced, 1922/64—water-colour

42. Klee, Silver Moon Chimes, 1923—water-colour

1923 //.2²   Stilleben ⟨mit d. Würfel.⟩

43. Klee, Still-life with the Die, 1923/22—water-colour

44. Klee, Moon Game, 1923/153—water-colour

45. Klee, Actor, 1923/27—oil on paper

46. Klee, Portrait of faded Beauty, 1924/11—oil on canvas

47. Klee, Dunes at Baltrum 1923/119—water-colour

48. Klee, Fishes—Aquarium, 1927/8—oil on gesso

49. Klee, Flora on the Sand, 1927/W 6—water-colour

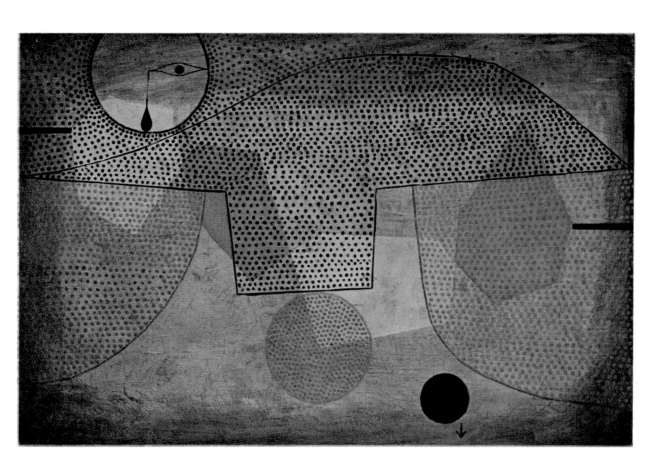

50. Klee, Sunset, 1930/E 9—oil on canvas

51. Klee, Relative Weights, 1930/3—water-colour

52. Klee, Last Snow, 1927/L 9—oil on canvas

53. Klee, Ghost with Glass and Dice, 1927/K 6—oil on canvas

54. Klee, A Shred of Community, 1932/X 2—water-colour

55. Klee, Limit of a Walk, 1933/H 8—water-colour

56. Kandinsky, Black Grid, 1922—oil on canvas

WASSILY KANDINSKY

At the outbreak of World War I in 1914, Kandinsky left Germany, which had been his second home for eighteen years. He returned in 1921, arriving in Berlin from Moscow at the end of December. During the period of the cultural upsurge immediately following the Bolshevik Revolution, he was highly respected in Russia as a pioneer and innovator. In 1918, he joined the Department of Art in the Commissariat for Popular Education and accepted a professorship at the State Academy of Art. After founding the Museum of Painting Culture in 1919, he organized twenty-two provincial museums in all parts of the Soviet Union in the course of the next two years. In 1920, he was appointed professor at Moscow University, and in 1921 he founded the Academy for the Study of Art. But even before the reaction of the early years of the Stalin era which ushered in a reactionary cultural policy, Kandinsky became disappointed with the direction the Bolshevik Revolution had taken; equally, he disappointed the Soviet art theoreticians, who later denounced him as the arch-enemy. He decided to give up his numerous official posts, and to turn his back on the U.S.S.R. The Communist philosophy was not his own, nor was he in sympathy with the artistic aims of the Constructivists, such as Tatlin and Malevich, in spite of apparent superficial similarities.

In 1922, Kandinsky provided one room of the 'Juryfreie' Exhibition in Berlin with full-scale designs for a mural painting, but, on the whole, he was repelled by the political ferment which dominated the postwar atmosphere in the German capital; perhaps it reminded him too strongly of the situation in Moscow. Kandinsky was therefore delighted at the prospect of working at the Bauhaus, particularly as he had a great affection for South Germany where, as a young man, he had found his artistic identity. The aims and methods of the Weimar Institute appealed to him. It would provide a peaceful setting where he could think and work with concentration, and there would be the other artists for whose work he had a high regard. For all these reasons, he gladly accepted the appointment, and arrived in Weimar in June, 1922, with his wife, Nina, whom he had married in 1917. He was fifty-six when he came to Weimar. There he met Klee whom he had known at Munich, and their friendship developed into a close co-operation which found its most fruitful expression in the mutually complementary courses of the two artists. In the catalogue of the Jubilee Exhibition held in Dresden on the occasion of Kandinsky's sixtieth birthday, Klee described their relationship:

> His generation matured before mine. I could have been his pupil, and in a sense, I was, for a word from him at various times helped and illumined my search. Needless to say, these words were backed by deeds (Kandinsky's early compositions). Then came what we did not believe we needed: the overwhelming reality of the European war, which brought, after a short reunion on a neutral island, the longer physical separation.

But the work continued steadily—over there for him, and here for the rest of us.... And today I say to him: Welcome! and move a little way towards him from the West. He comes a step in my direction, and my hand rests in his.

A gesture which truly spans the gulf between West and East. Kandinsky had always been the personification of dignity—a dignity based on a certain aloofness from emotional utterances, as well as on the consciousness of intellectual superiority, which established his dominance. With advancing age, this attitude intensified, and to his students at the Bauhaus he appeared as a distinguished-looking patrician with a solemn, professorial manner. His slightly leathery ram's face with its broad, strongly modelled features, had a distinctly oriental cast. He looked out with a searching gaze through rimless spectacles, while the studied elegance of his exterior suggested the scholar rather than the painter. In fact, he looked every inch the theoretician. His colleagues and friends could always sense the 'foreignness' of his mentality, even through the familiarity of intimate association. Lothar Schreyer wrote that he gave 'the impression of being a princely person, but not a European—rather a Mongolian prince'. (Schreyer, *Erinnerungen an Sturm und Bauhaus* [Memories of the Sturm and the Bauhaus], p. 232.)

This is how Georg Muche described Kandinsky's effect on others:

Seven versts is no great distance between friends. And Kandinsky put a distance of seven versts between himself and any friend who was close to him and to whom he wanted to be close. And he put seven versts between himself and a cause which meant anything to him. This is what gave him the superiority which distinguished him at the Bauhaus, and the equanimity which made him so trustworthy. The clarity of his thought, his judgment, and his language was coupled with an obliging smile, especially when he had to say no. Just as he sought a distance from the object in his pictures, so he tried to keep his distance from people. (Muche, *Blickpunkt,* p. 150.)

The impression Kandinsky made as a teacher has been described by his former pupil, Ursula Schuh:

After walking along the silent corridors, past closed doors bearing the imposing names of the famous, I come to the door which says 'Painting Class. Kandinsky.' Thank God, he has not arrived yet! I find myself a seat. Benches, desks, like a classroom. He arrives. Everything shadowy dissolves in a flash under this quick, bright-blue gaze through strong glasses. A gaze which takes an interest in everything. Which is perpetually solving new secrets. Then, before you know it, questions and answers plunge you right into the middle of his lesson on the theory of colour. He has brought with him a large number of rectangles, squares, discs, and triangles of different colours which he holds up in front of us in various combinations to test and educate our ability to see. For instance, in this combination, yellow is at the front and blue recedes. But if I now add this black, what happens? etc., etc. For the painter, it is a never-ending game, magic, but also torture—as when, for example, one cannot 'get it to the front.' It was only later that I noticed Kandinsky's mouth—of almost feminine sensitivity, though well controlled. His hair, streaked with grey. The dignity of his appearance, somewhat professorial. The correctness of his dark suit. The snow-white shirt, the bow-tie (like Braque's). Brown shoes. The soigné elegance of a scientist of 1931. Most fittingly, a certain impersonal attitude to people and things. With all this, very attractive. He might be well over 55, perhaps 60? This was the first and lasting impression which one received of Kandinsky as a person. ('*Im Klassenzimmer Kandinskys*' [In Kandinsky's Classroom], *Bauhaus Catalogue*, Frankfurt, 1964, p. 76.)

Wassily Kandinsky: The thin lines hold their own against the heavy point.
(From **Punkt und Linie zu Fläche**, Plate 9.)

At the Bauhaus, Kandinsky assumed the artistic direction of the mural painting workshop which had previously been the responsibility of Itten and Schlemmer in turn. His work there certainly left a stronger and more lasting mark than did Klee's activity in the bookbinding workshop. Later, Kandinsky also taught analytical drawing in the first term of the basic course. He took an interest in the Bauhaus Theatre directed by Schlemmer, and also tried his hand at several plays, some of which were produced at Dessau. However, the activity which had the most far-reaching consequence was Kandinsky's teaching on the theory of form and colour, which resulted in the publication of the treatise *Punkt und Linie zu Fläche* (Point and Line to Plane) as Bauhaus Book No. 9, in addition to many essays. All of this material was the direct outcome of his practical teaching.

There is a substantial consonance between the ideas propounded by Klee and those of Kandinsky, since the two friends' artistic philosophies are closely related. It can certainly be assumed that many of the thoughts they expressed in their lectures, had their origin in conversations between the two men. But their teaching methods were as vastly divergent as their characters were fundamentally different. Klee formulated his trains of thought with great care and caution, continually pointing out that whatever was right for him was not necessarily true for others. Kandinsky did not develop trains of thought; he postulated. He presented the end results of his deliberations, and declared: 'It is so,' precluding the possibility of other standpoints. As in mathematics, a proposition had to be either true or false. While Klee pursued the truth through all possible forms of the appearance of things, Kandinsky dictated laws. He was a dogmatist, a 'founding father' of the new art, who demanded absolute acceptance of his findings. In *Erinnerungen an Sturm und Bauhaus* (p. 233), Schreyer recalls how Kandinsky told him 'without presumptuousness but with the conviction of absolute certainty': 'The future has already begun. It is here now. It only needs a little courage by a few enlightened churchmen to ensure a place for twentieth-century art in the churches. But it is we who determine the art of the twentieth century.'

There is a story about a group of Kandinsky's students who were up in arms about his categorical assertion that in a picture, white was always at the front and black always at the back. They painted a white circle surrounded by black which, they explained, represented a view through a chimney, so that, in this case, white would be perspectively in the background. They took it to Klee and asked him to arbitrate. With a subtle smile, he said: 'White may be in the foreground, or again, it could also be in the background.' This anecdote illustrates the difference in attitude between the two teachers.

Writing to Otto Meyer-Amden on October 21, 1923, Schlemmer gave this ironic description of Kandinsky's teaching method:

> Kandinsky's lesson: rigorously scientific investigations into form and colour. Example: to find the appropriate primary colour for the three basic

forms (triangle, square and circle). It was decided that yellow stood for triangle, blue for circle and red for square, once and for all, as it were. (Schlemmer, *Briefe und Tagebücher*, p. 155.)

These episodes convey a lively impression of how Kandinsky must have appeared to students and colleagues at the Bauhaus—as an amiable though strict preceptor of absolute artistic laws, who was in the habit of formulating his assertions in concise dictums, as if they were codified legal decisions.

Kandinsky's outlook and philosophy were fundamentally determined by two factors: first, that he was a Russian; and second, that he had received legal training. As a Russian, Kandinsky inherited a long tradition which stands midway between European and Asian cultures and developed independently from the ethos of Central and Western Europe. Since the beginning of the fifteenth century, Central and Western European painting was committed to 'the only true faith' of the central perspective which can be scientifically calculated and which creates an illusionistic depth. Cézanne was the first Western artist to break away from this conception hallowed by tradition, which regarded art as the representation of an idealized existential environment. In Russian art, the central perspective was regarded as a Western influence which had been adopted comparatively late. Kandinsky, who grew up in an atmosphere of icons, where the significance of a painted picture was, in the first place, magical and not imitative, must have found it relatively easy to understand both the Oriental and the European conceptions in art. To him, therefore, central perspective was one of many forms of representation and composition. At the time of his arrival in Munich in 1896, he was not necessarily committed to the conception of illusionistic depth, and this inner freedom enabled him to detach the composition of a picture from its original content, regardless of perspective. Thus a new principle of autonomous composition was introduced into European painting, with far-reaching consequences. The decisive step toward abstract painting had now been taken. To the art world of the second decade of this century, it appeared astonishing and shocking and took a long time to establish itself with the general public.

Before Kandinsky decided to devote himself to art, he had followed a legal career, and this helps to explain his predilection for theorizing. In his artistic career, he distinguished himself as a theoretician and aesthetician as much as a painter. He possessed the ability to express his ideas and reflections in logically founded hypotheses and to formulate them clearly and coherently in the language of scientific discipline. This ability was of great advantage to him in his teaching, particularly as he had to find entirely new explanations for creative experiments for which no words had previously existed. His writings help one to understand his art. On the other hand, one might say that Kandinsky's paintings explain his writings by giving pictorial support to his theories. Kandinsky regarded himself as fulfilling the dual rôle of artist and art theoretician. This is what gave him the authority of his mission. Is it possible that in his heart he felt himself drawn more to theory than to practice? In *Point and Line to Plane*, he repeatedly emphasized that a reappraisal of aesthetic research would be necessary as a result of his findings, and he left no doubt that he considered himself in the first place as an innovator in the field of aesthetics. Many of his paintings can be likened to scientific trial-series, in which he carried out stylistic analyses of self-imposed formal problems. Through Kandinsky, painting has become a discipline which seeks to reconcile art and science in a method combining hypothetical postulate and practical experiment.

However, it was not only Kandinsky's Russian origin and his ability to think in abstract terms that moulded his personality structure; his individuality was marked by an unusual power of both eidetic and synaesthetic perception. These two faculties are connected, and they had a far-reaching influence on the form, direction, and extent of his artistic imagination.

Both eidetic and synaesthetic experiences are the result of an unusually intensive response to impressions. Most children have such experiences but lose them as they grow up. Kandinsky possessed the power of total visual recall; on occasion, certain external impressions could trigger off the reproduction of some long-forgotten experience in all its original intensity. Likewise, under the influence of some stimulus, his imagination could produce subjective impressions of a visionary kind—sudden, spontaneous experiences which had the same intensity as the experience of external reality. From this, Kandinsky learned that the inward reality of the mind can be experienced as concretely as objects of the outer reality, although there is a clear distinction between them. His realization of this process had a decisive influence on his development as an artist.

Kandinsky quoted many instances of this phenomenon in his autobiographical *Rückblicke* (Backward Glances), which was published by the *Sturm-Verlag* in 1913. For example, on arrival in Munich, he caught sight of a white dray-horse, which conjured up a lively memory of a white toy horse which had formed part of a racing game of his childhood. By this unforgettable experience, the whole of Munich was for him transformed into an enchanted city. Kandinsky describes another event of special significance which reflects this same visionary power. One evening, on entering his studio in the twilight, he could not immediately recognize one of his pictures, which was standing on the easel. For a brief moment, he was convinced he was seeing a marvellous absolute harmony of colours and forms, while the objective context of his own painting remained unrecognized. This visionary day-dream only lasted for a moment, then it was gone. But it means that Kandinsky had subjectively seen an abstract composition before he had actually painted the first one. Kandinsky says that he later lost this visionary ability, replacing it by other qualities in his painting. This may account for a certain hardness in his later style, when precisely calculated formal considerations replaced the spontaneity of his youthful power of experience.

Synaesthesia is the mental ability to experience sense-impressions of one kind by stimulus of a different sense or senses. Those who possess this ability will experience a corresponding colour tone when they hear a musical sound. For example, a given note will produce the impression of red of a certain brightness and intensity. This phenomenon has been investigated by a special branch of psychology called colour-tone research. From his own testimony, it is evident that Kandinsky was absolutely synaesthetic. In his autobiography, he describes a visit in 1899 to the Hermitage in St. Petersburg, where he experienced the chiaroscuro of Rembrandt's paintings as 'a giant concord'. About the same time, he was enraptured by a performance of *Lohengrin*, where he heard the same 'giant concord' at Wagner's trumpet sounds.

His series of woodcuts published by Piper in 1913 were entitled *Klänge* (Sounds), and in 1912, he published in the *Blaue Reiter Almanach* the draft of a first abstract stage play, with music by Arnold Schönberg. He called it *Der gelbe Klang* (Yellow Sound). It was the first occasion where an artist had tried to demonstrate on the stage a direct consonance between different sensory stimuli—colour, sound, movement—and also to demonstrate secondary temperature effects resulting from colour and sound, such as cold and warmth. This was intended to create a total experience of a certain kind in the audience, transferring sensory impressions into the emotional zone. Thus, Kandinsky tried to elevate his own strong experience—the consonance of the tones of music and colour—from the realm of subjective feeling to that of communication, from the private sphere into the general. He wanted to transfer the synaesthetic principle from the province of psychology to that of philosophy—albeit the philosophy of a painter. Kandinsky begins the sixth chapter of his book *Über das Geistige in der Kunst, insbesondere der Malerei* (Concerning the Spiritual in Art, and Painting in Particular) with a quotation from Delacroix: 'Musical sound acts directly on the soul and finds an echo there, since music is innate in man.' Further on Kandinsky explains:

> When the word red is heard, the colour is evoked without definite boundaries; if they are necessary, they have to be imagined deliberately. But red as is seen abstractly and not materially arouses both a precise and an unprecise impression on the soul, which has a purely internal physical sound. This red has also no independent transition to warmth or cold; the same must be imagined as subtleties of the red tone. Therefore, I call this spiritual seeing 'unprecise'. However, it is at the same time 'precise', since the inner sound remains without incidental tendencies to warm and cold, etc. This inner sound is similar to the sound of a trumpet or an instrument which one can imagine one hears when the word 'trumpet' is pronounced. This sound is not detailed.

From this definition of the 'inner sound', Kandinsky goes on to develop the 'principle of the inner necessity'.

Not surprisingly, such reflections eventually led Kandinsky to the conception of the *Gesamtkunstwerk* (integral work of art) based on synaesthesia. In his stage piece *Der gelbe Klang* (Yellow Sound), he tried to realize this ideal, although he was not entirely successful. In our century, Kandinsky is the artist who has done more than anyone else to propagate these ideas and to formulate them in detail with deep conviction and precision. But he was not the only one. Other artists had come upon the same relationships in the pursuit of their own aims. On commencing work at the Bauhaus, Kandinsky found many people who were receptive to his ideas—not only the musician-painters Feininger and Klee, but also Schlemmer, who had reached parallel conclusions in the sphere of choreography. Moreover, Itten's basic course, with its colour experiments, had prepared the students to look for conclusions similar to Kandinsky's own, although using different methods.

What they were all looking for was a system which would establish definite rules linking the different sensory perceptions and valid for all of them, as well as laws governing the conclusion that equivalent sensory perceptions are closely related in the reception centre of the mind.

Kandinsky tried to work out such a system in *Point and Line to Plane*. In the course of his endeavours in this field—as already mentioned—he allocated the colour blue to the form of the circle, red to the square, and yellow to the triangle. Kandinsky sought confirmation of his theses by means of a public-opinion poll, and distributed questionnaires asking for people's views on this subject. He also claimed that the direction of a line could be expressed in terms of temperature values: verticals mean warmth, horizontals cold. Black and white are silent colours: black corresponds to the horizontal, white to the vertical. A leftward direction expresses a tendency toward distance; direction to the right means homeward. He compared point and line in painting and the graphic arts with point and line in music and the dance, in an attempt to discover equivalent values of expression in different spheres.

When Kandinsky returned to Germany from Russia, his painting style was undergoing a crucial change. The Weimar Kandinsky was a different person from the Munich Kandinsky. According to Nina Kandinsky, the change in style came so suddenly that it caused confusion among art critics and connoisseurs alike, although they were used to dramatic changes in his work (*Vasily Kandinsky 1866–1944:* Catalogue of 1962 exhibition at Solomon R. Guggenheim Museum, New York, Supplement, p. 5). However, Kandinsky's development shows a sharp deflection rather than an abrupt break. The compact body of his early works is followed by the equally homogeneous late work. Nina Kandinsky calls the latter his 'architectonic phase', while Grohmann calls it 'the epoch of cool tectonic pictures' (Grohmann, *Wassily Kandinsky: Leben und Werk* [Wassily Kandinsky: Life and Work], p. 253), basing himself on a letter Kandinsky had written to him on January 31, 1924, in which he said: 'In 1921 began my cool period from which I emerge now and then.' (Grohmann, *Wassily Kandinsky*, p. 184.) However, the change is basically a reflection of his growing maturity. In the widest sense, one could define his youthful work of the Munich period as Romantic, and the later one of Weimar as Classical. A similar distinction can be made in the work of other artists, for instance Albrecht Dürer, or, in a different genre, Goethe. Kandinsky's seven years in Moscow—from the age of forty-nine to fifty-six—which preceded the new phase, and during which he produced comparatively few pictures, were certainly of great value as a pause for creative regeneration. Kandinsky's late period cannot be understood without his early work, on which it is founded.

Wassily Kandinsky was born in Moscow on December 4, 1866. His father, who was the son of a man banished to Eastern Siberia, was born at Kiakhta near the Mongolian border and became the director of a Russian tea company. In 1871, when Kandinsky was four, his family moved to Odessa. At the age of fourteen, he bought himself a box of paints, and his main hobby as a student was drawing and painting detailed interior and exterior views of Moscow churches. He began studying law and economics in Moscow in 1886, and he passed the state examinations in law in 1893. In 1889, he undertook a research expedition to the lake district of Vologda province, north of Moscow, on behalf of the Society for Natural Sciences, Ethnology, and Anthropology. There he studied the folk-art of the native peasant communities, and this journey made a deep and lasting impression on him. The Russians' close ties with their folk-art is evident in the work of many artists, for example, in the music of Stravinsky, Prokofiev, and Shostakovich. His experiences on this journey made Kandinsky acutely aware of this bond, and his feelings are described at great length in his autobiography. While living in Munich later on, he found that Bavaria was equally rich in folk-art, and the discovery of this similarity was a stimulus which found expression in the *Blaue Reiter Almanach*.

In 1896, he was offered a professorship at the University of Dorpat, which he declined. At the age of thirty, he decided to study art, and he moved to Munich, where he studied under Franz von Stuck at the Academy of Art from 1897 to 1899. In 1901, he founded the *Phalanx* group of artists and taught at the Phalanx School until he dissolved it in 1903. Meanwhile, he had met Gabriele Münter at this school, and in 1909, he set up house with her at Murnau in Bavaria. In the intervening years, his extensive travels included a journey to Tunis. He presided over the newly-founded *Neue Künstlervereinigung* (New Artists' Association). In 1910, he wrote *Concerning the Spiritual in Art, and Painting in Particular*, which was published by Piper in Munich in 1912. His friendship with Paul Klee and August Macke dates from 1911. With Franz Marc, he founded the Blaue Reiter, whose first exhibition was held at the end of the same year. In 1913, he exhibited in the First German Autumn Salon in Berlin, thus establishing contact with Herwarth Walden's Sturm circle.

Kandinsky's early efforts as a painter were filled with narrative bristling with romantic knights and castles. Against fairy-tale backdrops, he painted lively scenes with saints, warriors, pilgrims, merchants, and crinolined noblewomen. He designed these paintings on generous lines, preferring large spaces and strong colours. Even at this early stage, when his style was clearly influenced by *art nouveau,* he put his own individual stamp on it and revealed a tendency to abstraction, with pure colours and forms. The period of his early representational paintings was 1901–9. He produced his first abstract water-colour in 1910, although the actual transition to abstract painting was a gradual process. Kandinsky certainly did not invent abstract forms overnight, and at least until 1913, the connection with the object-bound motif remains manifest. Although at first glance the compositions may seem to be purely the play of form and colour, the figurative connection can be discerned when one looks at them with close attention. By calling his pictures 'Impressions', 'Improvisations', and 'Compositions', he made a deliberate distinction between them. The names serve to indicate the degree of spontaneity of their conception, as well as their origin. 'Impressions' give a new interpretation to impressions from the outside world, in which the original landscape character of the motif is still metaphorically recognizable. 'Improvisations' are the response to sudden intuitive ideas from the subconscious. 'Compositions' are carefully built up through a series of studies and sketches to the final polished work. The first works of this kind were an organic development of Kandinsky's previous style. In the multicoloured network of the pictorial structure, landscapes and figures are still decipherable, but their details are diffuse, as if hidden behind a veil. This style was notably represented by *Composition II* and the study for it (Grohmann, *Wassily Kandinsky*, p. 109), of 1910, in which one can at first see only patches of colour and lanes. On closer inspection, however, two men on horseback engaged in combat can be picked out in the centre, as in a picture-puzzle. A variation on the same motif was used by Kandinsky in *Composition IV* (Grohmann, *Wassily Kandinsky*, Plate 125), of 1911. Here, the reduction of the figurative motif to symbolic form has progressed further. The riders are engaged in combat on a rainbow-coloured bridge—perhaps chosen for its deeper associations: the rainbow could be an allusion to the transposition of the struggle from the world of reality to a spiritual sphere. Until 1913, Kandinsky incorporated in his work impressions which he had received from the landscape around Murnau, but at the same time, an iconographic plan unfolded in his mind. His recurring horsemen no longer signify romantic knights, but messengers between this world and the realm of the spirit. Kandinsky believed that an epoch was coming to an end in his time, and that the triumph of spiritual values was imminent. He as a painter felt the call to do his share in preparing for this event. Variations on messianic themes form the subject matter of his abstractions—the Flood, the Last Judgment, scenes from the Apocalypse, and the Easter theme of the Resurrection.

Kandinsky's messianic beliefs also emerge from several passages in his work *Concerning the Spiritual in Art, and Painting in Particular*. He refers to Russian authors hardly known elsewhere, but in this book he also deals with Goethe's theories, with which he found himself in sympathy. At that time, he was influenced by theosophy, and he quotes Madame Blavatsky and Rudolf Steiner. This influence must not be underrated, since certain aspects of the theosophical doctrine of salvation seem to corroborate Kandinsky's opinions to a very large extent. Klaus Brisch was the first to investigate Kandinsky's relationship with theosophy, and he drew attention to a theosophical theory of colour which was studied by Kandinsky and influenced his ideas on the nature of colour. (Brisch, *Wassily Kandinsky 1866–1944.*)

Kandinsky often spoke of his interest in the 'hidden' and the occult, which he wanted to reveal through his art. The hidden is like the unrecognized spiritual quality which is at work behind the exterior of things, and which becomes more and more evident as inner knowledge removes the obstacles of the material world. The artist recognizes the spiritual by listening to the laws of harmony which he carries within himself. Then he can follow what Kandinsky calls 'the principle of inner necessity'. In his book *Concerning the Spiritual in Art, and Painting in Particular*, Kandinsky, the great introvert, formulates general rules of subjective feeling which he has derived from intensive, disciplined self-observation. This book is an attempt to formulate as clearly as possible the metaphysics of the inner feelings. By educating the inner emotions, the principle of the inner necessity becomes self-evident. This is how the artist achieves his absolute spiritual freedom and comes to realize that art is superior to nature.

> I should like to remark finally that, in my opinion, we are fast approaching a time of reasoned and conscious composition, in which the painter will be proud to declare his work constructional—this in contrast to the claim of the Impressionists that they could explain nothing, that their art came by inspiration. We have before us an age of conscious creation, and this new spirit in painting is going hand in hand with thought towards an epoch of great spirituality. (Kandinsky, *Concerning the Spiritual in Art, and Painting in Particular*, p. 77.)

This was Kandinsky's artistic confession of faith before World War I. After the war and the Bolshevik Revolution, both his words and his pictures became more reticent. His language was as brilliant and polished as ever, but he no longer spoke with the tongue of a man who had seen the light of a revelation. He disciplined himself and formulated his theses in the exact language of scientific laws.

The figurative element in his paintings became increasingly difficult to decipher. The forms began to harden, to solidify, to become encrusted and encapsulated. Whereas they had previously been soft, fluid, and warm, they were now growing cold. These changes were foreshadowed in the relatively small number of paintings which he completed in Russia. In these pictures, Kandinsky's world had contracted and turned in on itself. The forms are encased in skins, and their chrysalis-like state gives a feeling of immobility. In the painting *Weisses Oval* (White Oval, Grohmann, *Wassily Kandinsky*, Plate 116), of 1919, a constricted beam holds the composition together; *Weisser Hintergrund* (White Background, Grohmann, *Wassily Kandinsky*, Plate 118), of 1920, is dominated by a strictly delineated tensioned bow. Here, precise forms with hard contours find their place in Kandinsky's painting for the first time. From 1921 onward, geometric elements proliferate until, in 1923, he begins to paint pictures which contain nothing else. From small, insignificant beginnings in 1920, clearly defined circles gain in importance and size as compositional accents, until they play a major rôle from 1923 onward. Kandinsky's paintings of the Bauhaus period are distinguished from his early works by the fact that the individual forms making up the composition as a whole have unambiguous contours and clear shapes which can be calculated with precision. It is now beyond doubt that the forms in his pictures are definite triangles, open angles, segments and circles, rectangles and polygons. Like parts of a building-set, the different components can now be enumerated, measured, and their relationship described with mathematical precision. The colours are contained and delimited by the shapes, and are no longer free to spill over into the surrounding zones. In this cool, tectonic style, Kandinsky's abstract painting has reached the stage of precise calculation; all the components—which in their relationship produce a pictorial tension—can be defined with great accuracy. Nevertheless, this stage was impossible without the preceding one; both have common roots.

On November 21, 1925—when *Point and Line to Plane* was just going to press—Kandinsky wrote to Grohmann, explaining his attitude to Romanticism:

I only wish people would understand what is behind my painting ... and not just content themselves with pointing out the fact that I use triangles or circles. I know the future belongs to abstract art, and I am distressed at the undue importance other abstract painters attach to mere questions of form. ... Form is for me only a means to an end, and I spend much time and intensive effort on the theory of form because I want to penetrate its inner mysteries. ... I was pleased to see you mentioning the word Romanticism. I do not want to paint tears for tears' sake, nor do I like sickly sweetness, but Romanticism goes far, far beyond the boundaries of tears. Today, there is a 'neue Sachlichkeit' [new objectivity]; there should also be a new Romanticism. I once felt like writing about this subject, and had thought of devoting one chapter of the new edition of *Concerning the Spiritual* to Romanticism. But in the meantime, the plan of my book has changed and it will appear in the form of separate

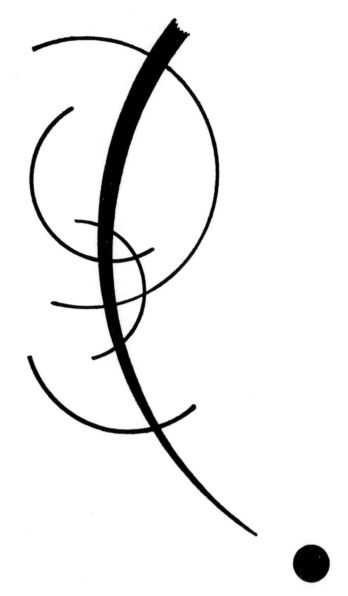

Wassily Kandinsky: Free curve versus point, with resonant geometric curves. (From **Punkt und Linie zu Fläche,** Plate 15.)

volumes. *Point and Line to Plane* is the first. It might be a long time before I get round to Romanticism. But what I do know is that modern man has a subconscious longing for Romanticism. Yet it is interesting to see the fear (*angst!*) the Germans have of this word. And the Russians too. This is something the two peoples have in common. The meaning, the content of art is Romanticism, and it is our fault if only one period in art is taken for the whole concept. ... I think it was in 1910 that I painted a Romantic landscape which had nothing to do with early Romanticism. I intend to use this term again some time. Up to now I have called a lot of things Lyrical Triangles (about which the press was unbelievably abusive),

Lyrical Construction, etc. But there is no longer the former gulf between the two terms: Where does one draw the line between Lyricism and Romanticism? The circle, which I have been using so often of late, is nothing if not Romantic. Actually, the coming Romanticism is profound and beautiful—the hackneyed word 'beautiful' must be used—it is meaningful, joy-giving—it is a block of ice with a burning flame inside. Too bad if people can only feel the ice and not the flame. But some of them are beginning to learn. (Grohmann, *Wassily Kandinsky,* pp. 180 ff.)

This passage is of particular significance because of Kandinsky's profound and searching analysis into his artistic motivation. For him, the meaning of Romanticism was much broader than the popular conception. By repudiating 'tears', he wanted to exclude the notion of sentimentality which is often loosely associated with Romanticism. His reference to the 'lyrical' shows that his idea of Romanticism served to refine the inner feelings and make them more receptive to the 'spiritual'. In 1925, Kandinsky was convinced that, however long it would take, the time could come when his views would be accepted. He constantly tried to overcome the lack of understanding for his art, which he encountered even from his friends, who could only see formal problems presented in circles and triangles. If he called his works Romantic, he certainly did not mean it in a narrow sense. He believed that his circles expressed Romanticism—a frozen Romanticism—and the description is apt. The content of Kandinsky's pictures of the 1920's seems to be frozen in rigid forms. Snow White was asleep in her glass coffin, and Kandinsky did not think the time was ripe to awaken her. What mattered to him was a reliable way of achieving the exact construction of a composition. This necessitated work with formal elements which could be strictly controlled. His method was analogous to the scientific procedure of conducting a series of trials to test various effects and reactions. Some of the experiments which Kandinsky conducted in his classes were not unlike modern psychological tests. Hence the cool character of his tectonic pictures. Nevertheless, the constructive façade concealed a blaze of emotions; or, rather, it enclosed these emotions the way the lustre of an insect trapped in amber is enclosed. This clear delineation of forms involved introducing into painting graphic techniques which had been disparaged since the Impressionists, who had placed so much emphasis on 'painterly' values. To answer criticism levelled against him from that quarter, Kandinsky wrote in *Point and Line to Plane:*

Even today, the use of the point or the line in painting is frowned upon by some art critics who would like to see certain old walls preserved, including that which until quite recently separated—apparently securely— two artistic fields, painting and graphics. However, there certainly is no fundamental reason for this separation.

During his Bauhaus period, Kandinsky painted a large number of pictures. He used to keep a handwritten catalogue of his works, and listed 3 paintings

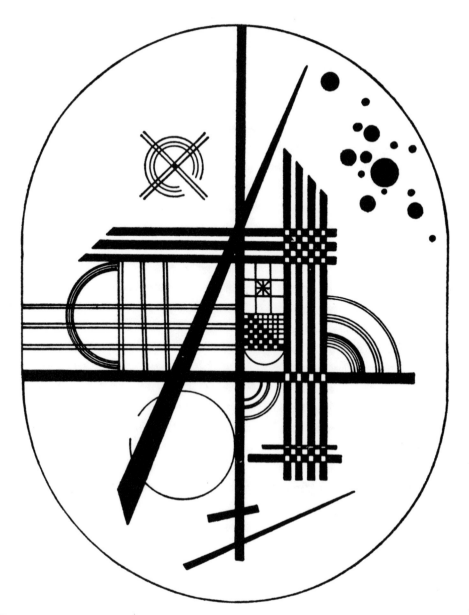

Wassily Kandinsky: Horizontal-vertical construction, with contrasting diagonal and tensions of points. Diagram of painting **Intime Mitteilungen** (Intimate Information), 1925.
(From **Punkt und Linie zu Fläche,** Plate 24.)

in 1922 (2 earlier ones still bear Russian titles); 19 in 1923; 29 in 1924; 34 in 1925; 49 in 1926; 43 in 1927; 24 in 1928; 52 in 1929; 54 in 1930; 27 in 1931; 13 in 1932; and the same number in 1933. Many of these paintings are grave and majestic in tone, some are lyrical, dramatic, or tragic. In a very few cases, they are pointedly comical but never—unlike Klee's works—ironical. There are no witty allusions to the human predicament, man's tragi-comic inability ever to attain creative perfection. To make a mockery of man's fall from grace was completely out of keeping with Kandinsky's serious-minded outlook. In fact, he attempted to convey in his compositions a feeling of cosmic perfection, creating on his canvases the strict harmony of complete micro-cosms, where all parts are gravitationally balanced in a perfect interrelation of size and mass. These clearly contoured, semigeometric shapes do not become fossilized; on the contrary, in their state of suspended animation, they achieve the tension of utmost elasticity and often give the appearance of stills from a dramatic sequence of movements. These hard-contoured forms are never found alone but are surrounded by diffuse backgrounds of subtly merging hues of colour. This duality brings about a vibrating counterplay of pictorial forces. One of his most beautiful paintings, *Einige Kreise* (Several Circles), of 1926, is an outstanding example of this style. It was formerly on permanent show at the Dresden Museum, but it was sold by the Nazis, who had confiscated it as 'decadent' art. It now belongs to the Solomon R. Guggenheim Museum in New York. This picture represents a cosmos of quiet harmony, consisting of larger and smaller circles of different colours which maintain their mutual gravitational equilibrium while floating in front of the muted background of a dark, honeycombed galaxy.

Point and Line to Plane, as Kandinsky emphasized, is a continuation of the ideas elaborated in his book *Concerning the Spiritual in Art, and Painting in Particular.* But *Point and Line to Plane,* which is the fruit of his practical teaching experience, is couched in a more concise and axiomatic language:

> The concept 'element' can be understood in two ways—the inner and the outer concept. In its outer meaning, every graphic or painted form is an element. In the inner concept, the element is not this form itself, but the tension which it contains. In fact, the content of a work of art is not determined by the outer forms but by the living forces alive in these forms = tensions. If these tensions were to disappear suddenly at the wave of a magic wand, or die, then the living work itself would be dead at once. If this were so, any accidental combination of forms would be a work of art. The content of a work is expressed in the composition, i.e. in the internally organized sum of its tensions. This seemingly simple statement is of great significance: its acceptance or refusal divides not only the artists but all men of today into two camps: 1. those who acknowledge the existence of the non-material or the spiritual, as well as the material, and 2. those who do not want to recognize anything beyond the material. For the second category, art cannot exist, and therefore, these people negate even the word art itself, and try to find a substitute for the word. (Kandinsky, *Punkt und Linie zur Fläche,* p. 27.)

In this spiritual credo, Kandinsky has given us an insight into the mainsprings of his own art. In this sense, *Point and Line to Plane* is a basic textbook. The geometric elements which he discusses—points, straight and curved lines, triangles, rectangles, circles, and the like—are not intended to be taken literally, but as symbols of emotions, which Kandinsky schematized so as to

57. Kandinsky, Composition, 1923—India ink and water-colour

58. Kandinsky, Bow and Point, 1923—oil

59. Kandinsky, On White, 1923—oil on canvas

60. Kandinsky, Dividing Line, 1923—oil on canvas

61. Kandinsky, Happy Mood, 1923—water-colour

62. Kandinsky, Upward Tension, 1924—water-colour

63. Kandinsky, Sharp Hardness, 1926—Oil on board

64. Kandinsky, Closely sourrounded, 1926—oil on canvas

65. Kandinsky, Upper Centre, 1926—water-colour

66. Kandinsky, Angular, 1927—oil on canvas

67. Kandinsky, Across and Up, 1927—water-colour

68. Kandinsky, Veiled Glow, 1928—oil on board

69. Kandinsky, Black-Red, 1927—oil on canvas

70. Kandinsky, Between the Light, 1931—oil on board

71. Kandinsky, Intermingling, 1928—water-colour

72. Kandinsky, Centre Blue, 1928—water-colour

73. Kandinsky, Circle and Spot, 1929—oil on canvas

74. Kandinsky, Thirteen Rectangles, 1930—oil on board

75. Kandinsky, Gentle Emphasis, 1931—oil on panel

76. Kandinsky, Pink Equilibrium, 1933—oil and tempera on canvas

make his argument more readily understandable. Kandinsky emphasizes that with these elements and their combinations, it is not a question of mathematical points and lines but of those qualities which the human mind can perceive through them. A circle which, mathematically speaking, would be a plane, can still appear to our eyes as a point, and it is difficult to determine the frontier where our senses convert a point into a plane. These are the problems the artist has to contend with, proceeding step by step from simple to progressively more difficult elementary combinations. *The Spiritual in Art* was a philosophy of sensibility based on metaphysics, whereas in *Point and Line to Plane,* Kandinsky worked out an exact mathematical system of the sensibilities by using forms borrowed from the realm of geometry.

It is difficult to gauge what ideological sacrifices Kandinsky had to make to achieve this schematic exposition. At any rate, it provided him with a didactic starting-point which enabled him to communicate his conclusions to the world. He caused the most profound revolution in art. At the same time, he steered art history and its terminology into unexpected new channels. This revolution is far from complete, even today.

Kandinsky remained faithful to the Bauhaus until the end. In 1925, he accompanied it to Dessau, where he lived in one of the newly-built masters' houses, next-door to Klee. After Gropius' departure, Kandinsky was the only one of the older generation of painters to continue under both Meyer and Mies van der Rohe. In 1932, after its closure at Dessau, he went with the Bauhaus to Berlin. When the Berlin-Steglitz Bauhaus was also dissolved, he considered the possibility of continuing teaching on a private basis. However, the unfavourable political situation drove him from Germany. He moved to Paris in 1933, where he lived in a flat at Neuilly-sur-Seine.

Kandinsky was now sixty-eight. The last picture he painted in Germany was called *Entwicklung in Braun* (Development in Brown). His first Paris picture, which he produced in 1934, he called *Start;* it marks the beginning of his late period. His late works are filled with a light-hearted gaiety which nevertheless makes timeless statements through graceful and whimsical gestures reminiscent of Chinese lyricism. The work of his old age is epigrammatic. Figures shaped like curving plant leaves appear frequently; an indefinable sweetness pervades them, in time they sink to the ground, overripe, heavy, and slack. In his last pictures, the shapes no longer interpenetrate or crowd in on one other, but are strung next to one another in neat rows. Many of them are surrounded by skins or encapsulated in boxes and tidily sorted into pigeon-holes. The arabesques which had flowered in Kandinsky's creative art during his long career found their way back into his spiritual coffers at the close of his life.

Kandinsky died at Neuilly-sur-Seine on December 13, 1944.

LASZLO MOHOLY-NAGY

In 1922, Gropius became acquainted with the work of the Hungarian Laszlo Moholy-Nagy and, as a result, invited him to teach at the Bauhaus. Moholy-Nagy arrived in Weimar in the spring of 1923 and took charge of the metal-work course. After Itten's departure, he also took over the basic course. Under his energetic leadership, the metal-work class developed into a disciplined work unit specializing in the design of modern everyday objects which were aesthetically pleasing and functionally perfected. The clean, elegant lines of lamps, saucepans, and many other household utensils later served as models for the design of mass-produced goods, and in this way the metal-work course has exerted considerable influence on the pattern of our contemporary domestic culture. Several leading industrial designers came from the ranks of apprentices and students of the metal-work class—Wilhelm Wagenfeld, Otto Rittweger, K. Jucker, Wolfgang Tümpel, and Marianne Brandt.

After Itten's departure, Moholy-Nagy carried on the basic course, having freed it from its ideological trappings. In particular, he continued the study of materials which, under his direction, acquired a more technical bias. The studies of balance which were undertaken in the basic course were completely in the spirit of Moholy-Nagy's stylistic concepts as expressed in his paintings.

Moholy was twenty-seven when he came to Weimar, and as one of the youngest Bauhaus teachers, belonged to Muche's generation. Photographs show him in an overall, wearing a peaked cap at a jaunty angle. His clear-cut features are those of *homo faber;* he looks more like a fitter than a painter. A comparison with Itten's photograph reveals the diametrical opposition of their mentalities: the engineer on the assembly line and the sorcerer in monk's habit.

In 1921–22, Theo van Doesburg who, with his friend Piet Mondrian, had founded *De Stijl,* was staying at Weimar. He was highly critical of the Expressionist tendency prevailing at the Bauhaus and tried to organize an effective opposition to it from the outside. In September, 1922, Van Doesburg convened an 'International Constructivist creative study group' at Weimar, with the object of creating an ideological alternative to the Bauhaus. On a group photograph taken at this congress, Moholy-Nagy can be recognized; he took part in its sessions as a representative of the Hungarian *Ma* group. Gropius had at one time toyed with the idea of calling Van Doesburg to the Bauhaus, but had been put off by his awkward character and had appointed Moholy-Nagy instead. This appointment may well have satisfied the other side of Gropius' personality, whose widely ranging intellect found inspiration both in the spirit of the medieval *Bauhütte* (masonic guilds) and in the functional clarity which typifies twentieth-century aesthetics.

Moholy arrived as Itten was leaving. Their spiritual polarity epitomizes the contrast between Weimar and Dessau. The formula 'Art and technology—a new unity' symbolizes the difference between Weimar and Dessau. It was rejected by Feininger, Itten, Muche, and Schreyer, while Schlemmer equivocated. Among the painters, Moholy was the first who expressly committed himself to it, and although he joined the teaching staff at Weimar, it is he who most consistently reflects the spirit of the Dessau Bauhaus under Gropius. Moholy was the first painter there who did not have the slightest interest in metaphysical problems and who did not spend his time pondering man's relationship with the beyond. This led to a certain amount of friction, and several early Bauhaus enthusiasts, blessed with more zeal than tolerance, totally misunderstood him. The picture of Moholy-Nagy conveyed by Schreyer is unjust, as there was no common ground between Moholy-Nagy, the technical pioneer, and Schreyer, deeply ensconced in his religious mysticism. (Schreyer, *Erinnerungen an Sturm und Bauhaus,* pp. 237 ff.)

Moholy-Nagy had the mentality of a pioneer who was fascinated and stirred by the dynamic pace of the machine age. His *élan vital* thrived on the tempo and the motorized rhythm of big-city life. His view of man was positivist, as can be seen from the following passage:

> Without attempting to solve all the imponderables of human existence, it can be said that man's structure is the synthesis of all his functional mechanisms. This means that man in each epoch is most perfect when his constituent functional mechanisms—both the cells and the most complicated organs—are developed to the limit of their potential capacity. This development is brought about by the arts. It is one of their major functions to establish new relationships between the known and as yet unknown visual, auditory and other phenomena and to compel the functional mechanisms to assimilate them. Man is unique in the insatiability of his functional mechanisms, which hungrily absorb every new impression and never cease to crave for more. This is one reason for the continuing need for the creation of new forms. But these forms can only have any value if they produce new, hitherto unknown relationships. Therefore, reproduction (i. e., the repetition of relationships already existing) must at best be regarded as a matter of mere virtuosity. Since creative production serves to extend man's development, we should strive to enlarge the scope of the means so far used only for reproductive purposes, so as to include productive purposes. (Moholy-Nagy, *Malerei, Photographie, Film* [Painting, Photography, Film], p. 23.)

This is Moholy-Nagy's artistic credo in a nutshell. Characteristically, he goes on from there to deal with photography, talking pictures, television, and the gramophone, all of which are media for the transmission of information. According to Moholy-Nagy, intellectual activity is a function of the human body which communicates information and sends out perceptions, reflexes, ideas, associations, symbols, and signals. Man is creative when his spirit creates new means of communication and new signalling symbols which lead to new and more differentiated combinations. Thus, the artist becomes a theoretician of communication. Moholy-Nagy's thoughts anticipated many ideas which were only collected after World War II into a new scientific discipline, that of cybernetics—a term which was coined by Norbert Wiener in 1948. Moholy-Nagy also touched upon the field of semantics—the science of the meaning and origin of signs and symbols—when he spoke of the 'new relationships between the known and as yet unknown visual, auditory and other functional phenomena' which art should endeavour to establish. On the other hand, Moholy-Nagy's thesis that 'man's structure is the synthesis of all his functional mechanisms' is closely related to the theory of the origin of human consciousness represented by dialectical materialism. In this connection, it is relevant to consider the conclusions which Pavlov arrived at in his experiments into animal response to stimulation. He distinguished conditioned and unconditioned reflexes which together form the 'first signalling system'.

In addition to this, there is the so-called 'second signalling system' consisting of words heard and seen. The second signalling system constitutes a higher order of response, radically different in quality from the response observed in animals. Words are stimuli similar to the signals of the first signalling system. However, their effect as stimuli does not depend on their visual or acoustic function, but on their content, their inherent meaning, through which they become signs and signals of certain objects or appearances which form the first signalling system. Therefore, Pavlov calls the word the 'signal of signals'. Thus, since the word forms a constituent part of the first signalling system, it is evident that in man these two systems do not function in isolation but are intimately related and interact. The second signalling system arises from the first and bears the same characteristics. According to Pavlov, the laws which determine the functioning of the first signalling system 'must also be valid for the second, which is subject to the same cortical processes'. Conversely, the existence of the second signalling system imparts to the first the character of conscious sensory response. 'Any response by the first signalling system is subsequently signalized by a new signal—the word—and becomes conscious. This conscious character of man's response essentially distinguishes his reflexes from those of animals. In order to emphasize this special character, it is called consciousness.' Through the existence of the second signalling system, Pavlov found another capability, a further new principle in cortical activity: 'Abstraction, involving at the same time the generalization of the countless signals of the second signalling system. . . .This principle establishes infinite orientation in the environment and forms the basis of man's highest adaptation—science.' (Gustav A. Wetter, *Sowjetideologie heute. Teil 1: Dialektischer und historischer Materialismus* [*Soviet Ideology Today*. Part 1: 'Dialectical and Historical Materialism'], Frankfurt, 1962, pp. 55 ff.)

tensions deriving from man's nature. The obvious differences in the art of various epochs are an expression of the fact that these relationships or tensions appear in different forms at various times in history. In practice, this means that a picture must have an effect simply through the harmony of its colours and the relationship of light and dark, irrespective of its so-called 'theme'. Therefore, even if a picture was stood upside-down, there would be sufficient basis for its evaluation as a painting. (Moholy-Nagy, *Malerei, Photographie, Film*, p. 9.)

Moholy-Nagy believed that the real purpose of art had at last been achieved, namely the representation of the tension-relationships determined by man's psychophysical apparatus. Both Moholy and Kandinsky painted abstract pictures, using geometrically definable and measurable forms. Yet their motivations were diametrically opposed. While both wanted to reveal inner, personal relationships, Kandinsky's outlook was fundamentally metaphysical—an attitude which was completely alien to Moholy-Nagy. His attitude to a painting might be likened to that of a graphologist toward a handwriting sample, or that of a psychologist toward an intelligence test. He was working for the establishment of generally valid rules (which could be incontrovertibly tested) governing the projection of psychomotor impulses as expressed in the relationship of tension, relaxation, and harmonization of forces. He believed that this had always been the function of painting, but that figurative representation had constantly suppressed and disguised the pure relationships. Now that photography had taken over the job of representing reality, the way lay open for a breakthrough to the 'isms' of pure painting.

Painters in all ages have striven to employ elementary optical means of expression. All known compositional rules of earlier painters—the golden section and other canons of pictorial construction—sprang from a basic human desire to maintain an elementary order and to express themselves in an elementary fashion. All the 'isms'—Impressionism, Neo-Impressionism, Pointillism, Futurism, Expressionism, Cubism, Suprematism, Neo-Plasticism, Constructivism—are nothing but reinforced individual interpretations of this immanent desire for organized order. The subconscious wish to elevate forms and colours into total optical means of expression, freed from their naturalistic carriers, has resulted in these styles with their deformation, fragmentation, dissolution of the object and distortion of its naturalistic image. (Moholy-Nagy, 'Ismus oder Kunst' [Ism or Art], *Vis voco*, Vol. V, No. 8/9, Leipzig, August—September, 1925. Quoted in Wingler, *Das Bauhaus*, p. 124.)

Moholy-Nagy spoke of easel painting as pigment painting. Most of his pictures were painted on canvas, and he often left part of the canvas fabric bare, to add texture interest. He tried to paint on synthetic resin plates to achieve novel and subtle colour effects. He felt that the future of painting techniques lay with synthetic materials and surfaces—a prophecy which has, to a certain extent, come true already.

Those who see some kind of machine art in his pictures are misjudging him. Each composition is a highly sensitive balancing act. His interest in kinetic-optical processes is manifest in his pictures. In every one of them, an optical movement has come to rest in a state of precarious equilibrium. His compositions are based on straight lines varying in thickness from knife-edge lines to broad beams, crossing and intersecting, together with circles, triangles, rectangles, parallelograms, and trapezes. Moholy-Nagy employed economy of means not only in his composition, but also in his colour effects. He applied colour thinly, and strong colours were reserved for major compositional accents. Large surfaces are painted in delicate hues, frequently translucent and giving an impression of angular glassy planes. None of Moholy-Nagy's compositions consist of verticals and horizontals alone, which are, after all, imposed by the picture edges. He preferred all the variants of the diagonal, which he placed in meaningful relationship to the outside edges of the composition. Thus he achieved—again with great economy of means—the utmost pictorial tension. Whenever horizontals and verticals were included in a composition, he would place added emphasis on diagonal relationships. Diverging systems of co-ordinates are brought into a carefully balanced relation.

Moholy-Nagy gave his pictures neither objective nor symbolic titles, but named them with numbers and letters. His painting *Z III*, of 1922, consists of four circles—a large, pale yellow one, a smaller pink one, a small blue one, and a very small one of glowing yellow. The smaller the forms the more luminous the colours. To these, he added two broad bright-red beams crossing diagonally, and six intersecting straight hair-lines. A total of three different formal elements appear in twelve individual modalities. None of them touch the picture edge. With these strictly limited means, Moholy-Nagy achieved a sureness of expression which gives the composition the exactness of a formula.

Moholy-Nagy maintained that photography had taken over from painting the task of providing a realistic representation of our environment. When the painter no longer used the camera mechanically, merely to make a visual record, but began to use it for conscious creation, he elevated the technique of photography to an art form.

> The creative use of these insights and principles will silence once and
> for all those who maintain that photography is not 'art'. The human
> spirit constantly opens new fields for creativity. In photography too,
> we shall see a great upsurge in the near future. As an art form, photog-
> raphy does not merely copy nature. The scarcity of 'good' photographs
> proves my point. Out of millions of photographs used to illustrate books,
> only a very few can be regarded as really 'good'. What is interesting,

and supports my contention, is the fact that our long tradition of 'seeing' enables us to pick out with unfailing instinct those photos which are 'good', regardless of their novelty or thematic originality. There is a new qualitative appreciation of light-dark contrasts, of brilliant whiteness, of the fluidity of light seen in transitions from black to grey, of the magical exactness of the most delicate fabric, of the skeleton of a steel structure and the spray of the ocean waves—all of which can be captured in a hundredth or a thousandth of a second. Feeling for material + economy = beauty = modern riches. (Moholy-Nagy, *Malerei, Photographie, Film*, p. 26.)

This is how Moholy-Nagy discovered creative photography. Together with Man Ray, he is today considered one of the founders of photographic art. Moholy-Nagy's achievements made it possible to class photography as a new artistic discipline, and museums should recognize it as a suitable subject for collections before it is too late. Admittedly, pressure on a trigger as technical mediator between spirit and hand is still regarded with a certain scepticism; nevertheless, it is now generally accepted that artistic quality does not depend on the length of time spent on a work or on perfect craftsmanship, but on originality of perception.

In *Malerei, Photographie, Film*, Moholy-Nagy illustrated his thesis with the work of other photographers, as well as with his own. His interest ranged far beyond glimpses of our mundane environment, into the manifold possibilities developed by him and others through new techniques—microphotography, macrophotography, the photogram, overexposure, trick photography, double exposure, imaginative use of the developing process, the photo negative, photomontage, photography in advertising, Viking Eggeling's abstract cartoon films, and the cinema as a whole, with its uncharted potential.

In 1930, Franz Roh published a volume of sixty photographs by Moholy-Nagy. It is not only Moholy-Nagy's technical mastery and his use of montage and other techniques that make the photographs artistically significant; it is also his completely novel and individual manner of looking at familiar things—the use of bold foreshortening, unusual angles, and superimposed light-dark structures, such as the shadow of a net or a fence, imbues his portraits and objects with a mysterious quality.

Moholy-Nagy's photographic *tours de force* met with resounding success at the Bauhaus. Inspired by his example, the students enthusiastically took to their cameras. Moholy-Nagy's wife Lucia took photographs, Muche took photographs, and many an unsuspected talent came to light among the students, including Feininger's son Lux, and Paul Citroen with his 'city' montages. These Bauhaus experiments had an extraordinary influence on the development of advertising techniques. It was only in 1929, some time after Moholy-Nagy's departure, that a regular course in photography was instituted at the Bauhaus under the direction of Walter Peterhans.

Moholy-Nagy created designs for a new, revitalized typography. In this he was inspired by the same basic conception of 'producing new, partly unknown relationships, and correlating them with old-established functional relationships'.

Script is one of the most precise means for the communication of ideas, complexes of ideas, and messages. Script is a small and easily assimilated store of unequivocal elementary signs, which can be put together in an infinite number of combinations to express every imaginable statement. Printed script, moreover, has the advantage of being fixed in unchanging forms. For all these reasons, Moholy-Nagy felt himself drawn to typography. He wanted to intensify the informative and aesthetic value of typography by increasing its communicative power with simple and impressive signalizing elements which almost raised it to the level of graphics. He contended that printing processes had not undergone a significant change, either technically or aesthetically, since Gutenberg's time, and that the printed image should be made lively and interesting and should be brought up to date to make it worthy of the twentieth century. To this end, he envisaged the addition of accents and direction signs functionally derived from typographic forms and rules—not only for single words and sentences, but for the whole printed page. In an essay written in 1924 and published two years later, Moholy-Nagy wrote:

> Typography is contemporary if it uses formative means which are the logical outcome of its own order. ... Work today inevitably involves modern technology and the use of machines. To express the character of the technological age, contemporary products of the printing industry will have many points in common with the latest machines, i.e. they will have clarity, compactness and precision. ... Typography depends on the effectiveness of optical relationships. Every period has its own optical norm which finds expression in its typography. The lively type-face full of contrasts, which we find in old printed works, has degenerated into the rather monotonous grey of later books resulting from the tremendous expansion of printing processes and the great demand for print which was accompanied by an economic and lucrative use of paper, small format, linotype, monochrome print, etc. The monotonous appearance of modern books has some disadvantages: firstly, even with the use of paragraphing, a clear arrangement of the text is difficult; secondly, the reader tires far more quickly than when he is faced with a page alive with contrasts of colour and tone. ... Opportunities for innovations in typography are constantly developing, based on the growth of photography, film, zincographic and galvanoplastic techniques. The invention and improvement of photogravure, photographic typesetting machines, the birth of neon advertising, the experience of optical continuity provided by the cinema, the simultaneity of sensory experiences—all these developments open

the way for an entirely new standard of optical typographic excellence; in fact, they demand it. The grey text will give way to a coloured picture book, to be experienced as a continuous visual event (the connected sequence of many single pages). With the progress of reproduction techniques, probably all works, even on philosophy, will use such means of illustration. (Moholy-Nagy, 'Zeitgemässe Typographie—Ziele, Praxis, Kritik' [Contemporary Typography—Its Aims, Practice, and Critique]. *Offset, Buch und Werbekunst*, No. 7 [Bauhaus], Leipzig, 1926. Quoted in Wingler, *Das Bauhaus*, pp. 95 ff.)

We have not quite reached this stage yet! However, Moholy-Nagy's theories have been adopted and put into practice everywhere, and his ideas have become common property. He designed many prospectuses, dust jackets, and layouts of books published by the Bauhaus. He reformed and simplified the type elements themselves: for example, letters, numbers, punctuation marks, directional arrows, borders, and the like. Words and complete sentences were emphasized by double-spacing or bold type. The printed page was transformed into a conscious system of varied and related accents. In his page layout, he made use of different-sized letters, varying degrees of boldness, and unusual arrangements in horizontal and vertical patterns. The object was to catch the eye in a dramatic manner. Moholy-Nagy's solutions were often quite startling, and in some of his typographic pictorial language one can almost hear the ringing of alarm bells. The trend inspired by him at the Bauhaus was later developed by Josef Albers and Joost Schmidt.

While still at the Bauhaus, Moholy-Nagy worked on a problem which was to occupy much of his energy later—an optical-kinetic sculpture which he called 'space modulator'. It is a curious contraption made up of the most diverse materials, a 'functional apparatus' which looks like the embodiment of his philosophy. With these space modulators, he pioneered a new art form which was later explored again by Jean Tinguely and the *Zero* group of artists.

Moholy-Nagy left the Bauhaus in 1928, when Gropius resigned. He first went to Berlin, where he designed stage sets for the State Opera House and the Piscator Theatre. He subsequently engaged in experiments with photography and the cinema. He went to Amsterdam in 1934 and to London in 1935, where he continued his work on his space modulators. In 1937, he founded the New Bauhaus in Chicago. The school was not financially viable and had to close down shortly after its inception. In 1938, he opened the School of Design.

Moholy-Nagy died of leukemia in Chicago on November 24, 1946.

77. Moholy-Nagy, The Great Emotion Machine, 1920—oil on canvas

78. Moholy-Nagy, The Large Railway Picture, 1920—oil on canvas

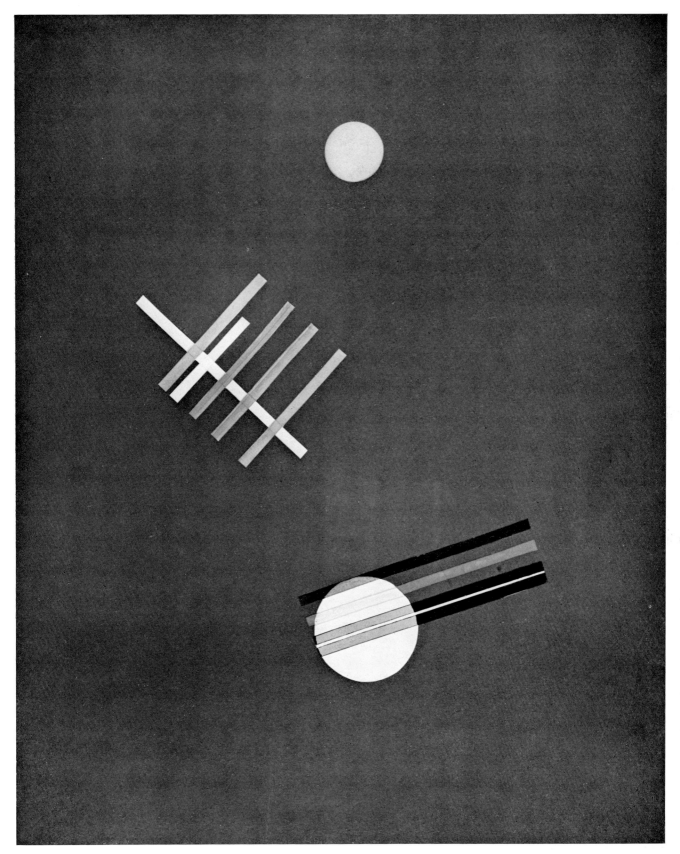

79. Moholy-Nagy, KL 8, 1922—Collage on red paper

80. Moholy-Nagy, A XX, 1924—oil on canvas

81. Moholy-Nagy, Q IV, 1923—oil on canvas

82. Moholy-Nagy, Z VIII, 1924—oil on canvas

83. Moholy-Nagy, Z III, 1922—oil on canvas

84. Bayer, Cloudscape, 1928—gouache

85. Bayer, Timber in the forest, 1930/13—water-colour

86. Bayer, Abstraction, Blue-Composition in Space, 1928/11—water-colour and gouache

87. Bayer, Clouds and Frames, 1928/11—gouache

HERBERT BAYER

When former Bauhaus students were given teaching posts at Dessau they were known as 'young masters'. As such, Josef Albers became head of the basic course, Marcel Breuer took over the carpentry course, Hinnerk Scheper the mural painting workshop, Joost Schmidt the sculpture workshop, and Gunta Stölzl the weaving department.

Herbert Bayer joined the teaching staff in 1925, at the same time as the other 'young masters'. He took charge of the print shop. These teachers, who had risen from the ranks of the students, helped to create the working atmosphere characteristic of Dessau, where the exaltation typical of Weimar was replaced by a more objective attitude. Herbert Bayer worked as a painter, typographer, advertising designer, and photographer. His activities in advertising influenced the style of his other work. His paintings, water-colours, and drawings embody a restrained 'drawing-board' Surrealism. Some of the devices which he used as formal elements to achieve his artistic effects bear the unmistakable imprint of advertising techniques.

Herbert Bayer was born at Haag in Upper Austria on April 5, 1900. He went to school at Linz and served in the Austrian army from 1917 to 1919. In 1919, he enrolled at a studio of applied arts at Linz. In 1920, he was engaged as assistant to the architect Werner Margold, in the artists' colony at Darmstadt. From 1921, Bayer studied at the Bauhaus, particularly in the mural painting department under Kandinsky. Nevertheless, his work shows the influence of Moholy-Nagy rather than Kandinsky, and it was at this time that he became interested in problems of typography. In 1923–24, he went on a long trip to Italy. On his return, he worked as a painter in Berchtesgaden until he was appointed to the Bauhaus.

In 1925, Bayer painted a tempera picture entitled *Komposition im Raum* (Composition in Space, Bayer-Gropius, *Bauhaus 1919–1928*, p. 202). On a horizontal board, foreshortened in perspective, it shows light-coloured and translucent slablike shapes—triangles, rectangles, wavy strips—arranged according to shape and lined up one behind another like flats in a stage set. Some stand on the board and others hover above it in a mysterious gravitational relationship. The rhythmic repetitive order fades as it recedes, and comes to an abrupt halt against a background of unfathomable darkness. Both as a whole and in many of its details, the composition resembles Paul Klee's fugue pictures. However, Bayer did not borrow the idea from Klee; it can be assumed that both were inspired by the experimental films of Hirschfeld-Mack. In fact, Herbert Bayer's painting is an almost exact reproduction of one phase of these coloured-light films, which owed their effect to the play of light produced by stencilled figures. On the other hand, Klee's comparable pictures showed a greater individuality in the adaptation of the same theme.

The layered construction which, in this picture, appears in pure form, can also be found in many of Bayer's other compositions, suggesting theatrical scenery. His pictures create a quiet, brittle world which, despite its restraint, produces an uncanny feeling. The small stage on which the action takes place seems to end in nothingness, and the background presses so closely forward that there is little space left for the objects, which become flattened like plants preserved in a book. The world is depicted in a series of abstractions collected in a picture album with transparent pages. Every time a page is turned, the perspective changes, revealing varying levels of reality. This idea of super-imposing and removing layers of designs corresponds to an architect's working method. In Bayer's world, objects are placed next to one another in flat planes. The clouds on the horizon at the back are filtered through a series of picture frames, until their disembodied contours are reproduced in the nearest frame as on a sheet of transparent paper. The trees are shaped as if by a fret-saw. The immeasurable has been squashed flat to make it measurable; an introvert has brought neatness and order into the absurd.

Bayer's work in advertising and typography has probably had more impact on the social scene than his 'pure' paintings and water-colours. Like Joost Schmidt, Bayer was inspired by Moholy-Nagy's ideas and developed them further, bringing under control some of his wilder flights of imagination. Bayer may also have been influenced by *De Stijl*. He designed new type-faces, printed forms, and letterheads for the Bauhaus. He promoted the Grotesque series of founts—now in general use—and, among other things, designed a 'shadow-script' without outlines, which simulates the shapes of letters in relief. He wanted to explore the causes of typographic impact scientifically rather than intuitively.

> The design of advertising matter means more than just tasteful artistic layouts. . . . A really objective approach to this subject means that external appearances must be related to essential content, and this must be understood before work begins. . . . Effective advertising design should be based, first and foremost, on the laws of psychology and physiology. At the moment, advertising is largely a matter of intuition. Consequently, it is impossible to calculate success with any certainty or to define one's aims with precision. (Herbert Bayer, 'Typographie und Werbesachen-gestaltung' [Typography and the Layout of Publicity Material]. *Bauhaus*, Vol. II, No. 1, Dessau, 1928. Quoted in Wingler, *Das Bauhaus*, p. 144.)

In his advertising copy and layouts, Bayer used contrasting effects with a Surrealist flavour, combining two- and three-dimensional effects with the resources of photography and typography. He specialized in new forms of display for exhibition pavilions, and designed an architecture appropriate to their particular function. He also designed printed forms, magazine covers, posters, invitation cards, bank notes, and many other things. The advertising style which was developed in the late 1920's and is now taken for granted almost everywhere owes some of its most important ideas to Herbert Bayer.

Like Moholy-Nagy, Bayer left the Bauhaus when Gropius resigned. From 1928 to 1938, he worked in Berlin as painter, photographer, typographer, and advertising and exhibition designer. He emigrated to America in 1938. In New York, he was retained as a consultant by Wanamaker's Department Store and the J. Walter Thompson Advertising Agency. He was appointed Director of Art and Design by Dorland International, for whom he had previously worked in Berlin. He played a vital part in the staging of the great Bauhaus exhibition of 1938 at the Museum of Modern Art. In 1946, he moved to Aspen, Colorado, where he now lives. He collaborated with Gropius in the preparation of the book *Bauhaus 1919—1928,* which was published in Boston in 1959.

JOSEF ALBERS

Of all the painters at the Bauhaus, Josef Albers spent the longest period there, first as a student and later as a teacher. Like Herbert Bayer, he was appointed a 'young master' in 1925 and belongs to the circle of former Bauhaus students. He studied at Weimar from 1920 to 1923, when he took charge of the technical direction of the glass workshop. In addition, he taught practical workmanship to the basic-course students. After the move to Dessau, he received full staff status and continued his previous activities until Moholy-Nagy's departure, when he became head of the basic course. In addition, he directed the furniture workshop from 1928, in succession to Marcel Breuer. Albers remained at the Bauhaus until it was closed down in 1933. He developed a puritanically rigorous Constructivist style, which achieved its aims by the use of a few, clearly differentiated formal elements. This style epitomizes the constructive-functional character of Dessau as opposed to the metaphysical trend of the Weimar period.

Josef Albers was born at Bottrop in Westphalia in 1888. He studied at the Royal Academy of Art in Berlin from 1913 to 1915, and at the Essen School of Arts and Crafts from 1916 to 1919, followed by a year at the Munich Academy of Art. He then became a student at the Bauhaus, specializing in stained glass, a field in which he developed new means of expression. He made stained-glass windows for the Sommerfeld House in the Berlin suburb of Dahlem, for the Dr Otte House at Zehlendorf, and for the staircase of the Ullstein publishing house. These early works already betray his predilection for arrangements of mainly rectangular, harmonically related forms. In later years, his style became even more precise, particularly in his opaque wall pictures made with layers of glass fused together in the so-called thermometer style by a technique invented by him, which required meticulous care. In his artistic experiments, he made use of simple, clearly delineated elementary forms. They were mostly long, narrow rectangles brought into vertical and horizontal interrelationships, thus symbolizing the basic structure of our optical-spatial orientation. Unlike Moholy-Nagy, who emphasized diagonals, Albers preferred verticals and horizontals in echelon formation. Nevertheless, as a secondary function of this arrangement, the diagonal is an essential element in his compositions. The construction of these compositions runs parallel to the picture frame. Many variations of an ever-changing screen pattern result from the displacement, transposition, and alignment of identical or similar formal components, which show a serial difference in their proportions of length. Reduced to bare essentials, this distribution of verticals and horizontals represents a variation on the axial cross. His compositions fit into a firm harmonic system, as if he were playing fugues on the keyboard of his 'optical piano'. Colouring is limited to simple contrasts, mostly black and white, with occasionally one supporting colour. Up to three interlocking rhythmical elements are employed, each being distinguished by its colour composition and the value of its individual symbols. This system gives the impression of a vibrating pattern. It is spread out like a musical score, and there is a feeling that it could conceivably be read and played. Some of Albers' sayings are formulated as concisely as those of Lao-tse, and the same compactness of expression characterizes his pictorial art.

The series of formal experiments undertaken by Albers under laboratory conditions with deliberate limitation of means are analogous to experimental practices in the exact sciences. His method of basic research in art has found many followers, especially in the United States, and Albers is now recognized as one of the pioneers of 'concrete art'. A number of important artists are to be found among his former students. A revitalized concrete art, reverberating from America to Europe under the name of Op Art, owes much to the ideas Albers has been propagating through his work and teaching in America. 'Construction means planning, organizing, classifying, comparing and controlling. In other words, it comprises everything opposed to disorder and chance. This is why it fulfils a human need and is basic to man's thought and action.' (Bucher, *Josef Albers: Trotz der Geraden* [Defiance of the Straight], p. 75.)

Two principles guided Albers in his teaching at the Bauhaus: first, that the artist should create the form of an object with the minimum number of tools; and second, that as little as possible—ideally, nothing—should be lost of the quantity of material at the artist's disposal, nor should he add to it afterwards. True artistic ability should prove itself in the utmost economy of means. The results achieved in Albers' course by following these principles were, indeed, astonishing. Albers demanded a working material which would be both simple and adaptable. In his courses, therefore, pride of place was given to the cutting and folding of paper—a material which can be considerably changed in form with very little manipulation. The paper was examined for resistance to pulling and tearing, for its architectonic stability and other typical properties. From paper alone, by a sequence of logically planned, simple manipulations, the students created impressive spatially sculptured structures, without adding to or taking away from the quantity of material available at the outset. This proved that it was possible to change the qualities of an object consisting of a given limited material simply by altering and re-organizing its form. This was a discovery of philosophical significance. Reliefs made from paper had differing structures, textures, and light-and-shade effects, so that they sometimes looked like models of modern housing estates. Other experiments consisted of twisting strips of paper in spirals to see how the originally parallel strips were affected by the altered spatial relationship. There were also experiments with the displacement of typographic patterns.

Albers has described what he hoped to test and achieve by his teaching, and the following passage illustrates the essential change which had been wrought in the basic course since Itten's time, despite external similarities.

In addition to economy in materials, we practise economy of effort. This is encouraged by the study of quicker, easier working methods, by the use of versatile materials, and of ready-made and easily available components, by the judicious choice of tools, and by ingenuity in improvisation. The rationalization of several work processes into one unified process, restriction to one tool or one work process, the emphasis on economy of labour only seem to contradict the digressive methods demanded by teaching. In practice, actual shortening of work processes does not begin until later. By clarifying this apparent contradiction, one elicits the difference between factory and educational methods.... A sociological economy must reject the personality cult prevalent in present-day educational methods: productive individuality asserts itself without and against education. Another sphere of work with opportunities for free creativity presents itself in the so-called 'exercises in the study of matter'. These alternate throughout the term with the 'exercises in materials'. 'Exercises with matter' are concerned more with the external appearance than the inherent energy of working materials. A relationship is established between the 'skins' of the materials.... General discussions about the results of exercises with both matter and materials are followed by more precise observation and re-education of the eye. These discussions bring to light our actual formal requirements: harmony or compromise, rhythm or measure, geometric or arithmetic proportions, symmetry, asymmetry, rosette or row. This in turn brings us to the more vital questions: enrichment or austerity, complicated or elementary form, unison or polyphony, mysticism or hygiene, volume or line, beauty or intellect, ancestral portrait or W.C. ... To sum up, the aim of the inductive teaching method outlined above is to induce in the student responsibility and discipline towards himself, the material and his work, and to enable him to recognize the line of work and materials in which he could do the most satisfactory work. This teaching method will increase the student's understanding by compelling him to submit his work to constant systematic analysis, in the light of his actual experience. It aims at training a wide mobility, so that later, necessary specialization does not isolate the artist's work from the mainstream. It leads to economy of form.
(Josef Albers, 'Werklicher Formunterricht' (Practical Instruction in the Making of Forms), Bauhaus, Vol. II, No. 2/3, 1928. Quoted in Bauhaus Catalogue, Frankfurt, 1964, pp. 118 ff.)

The insights Albers gained from his studies of material, form, structure, and texture found practical application in his design of furniture and other articles for use where their basic aesthetic and functional purposes were carefully considered. Even before taking over the carpentry workshop, he often used to work there. In 1923, while still a student at Weimar, he designed a church pew which was shown at the Bauhaus exhibition that year. Under his direction, the

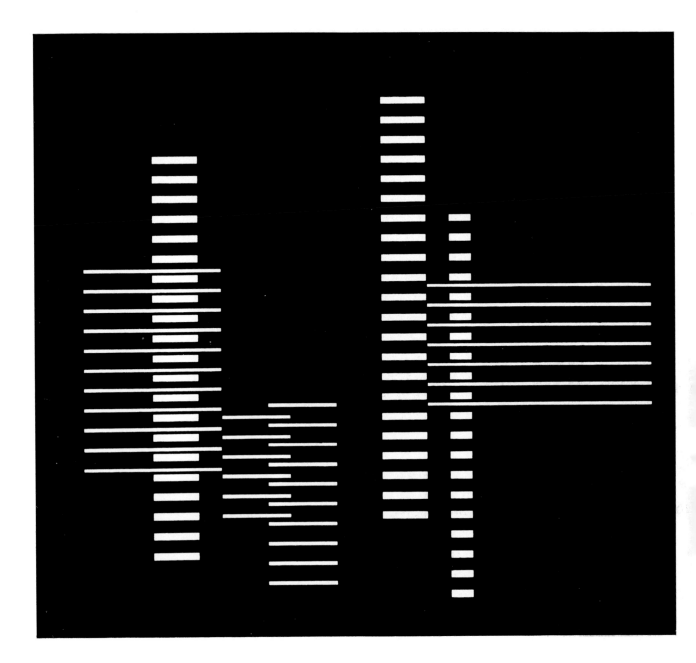

88. Albers, Tall Buildings, 1927—glass

89. Albers, Glass Window—glass

90. Albers, Bundled, 1925—glass

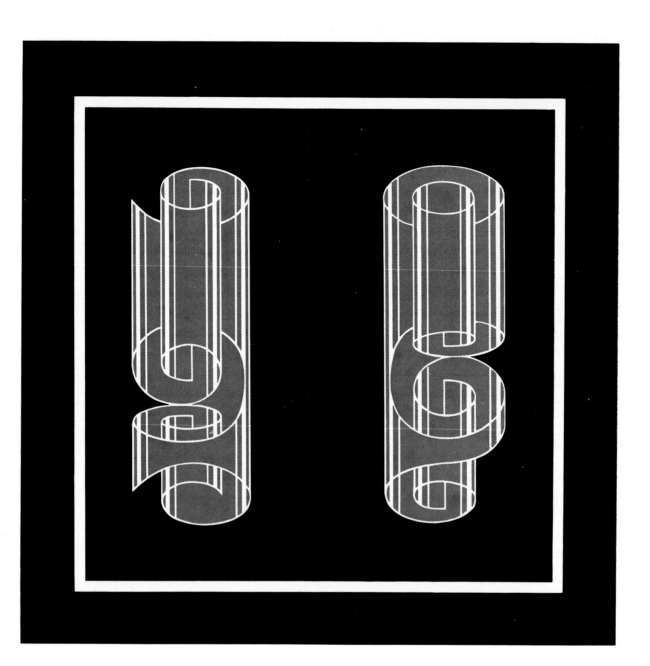

91. Albers, False Coil II, 1931—glass

carpentry department produced models of simple, attractive, yet inexpensive furniture for mass production. Albers created an armchair in wood and metal, easy to assemble and take apart, which was rationally constructed with optimum economy of materials.

Like his colleagues Herbert Bayer and Joost Schmidt, Albers also worked on the reform of typography. In 1926, he designed a stereotyped alphabet composed of simple geometric forms—the half-circle, the quarter-circle, the rectangle, and the square. Its block effect, visual impact, and great legibility made it particularly suitable for advertising purposes. Albers was interested in schematizing and rationalizing the printed image, and there was a constant exchange of ideas between him and his friends.

After the dissolution of the Berlin Bauhaus in 1933, Albers was the first of its artists to emigrate. On the recommendation of the Museum of Modern Art, he went to the United States, where he took up an appointment at Black Mountain College in North Carolina. He remained there until 1949, and during this period he also conducted summer courses at Harvard University. In 1949 and 1950, he was visiting lecturer at the Cincinnati Art Academy, Yale University, the Pratt Institute of Art in New York, and the Harvard summer school. In 1950, he became a professor at Yale University, where he was the head of the Faculty of Art. He has given guest lectures in Mexico, Cuba, Chile, Peru, Hawaii, and at the Academy of Creative Art at Ulm in Germany. Albers now lives in New Haven, Connecticut, where he is continuing his research and experiments into the fundamentals of creative form.

The seeds of German culture have been scattered to the winds. The barbarism of Nazism drove out the most eminent representatives of the German spirit. They took their knowledge, their experience, their philosophy, and their imagination with them to other countries, where the fruits were harvested. The Germany of today is justly diminished by this loss. The irony of history has fittingly rewarded the lust for power.

It is not only the physical sciences that suffered, but art, too. The following Bauhaus masters emigrated to the United States: Walter Gropius, Ludwig Mies van der Rohe, Lyonel Feininger, Laszlo Moholy-Nagy, Herbert Bayer, Marcel Breuer, and Josef Albers.

Albers taught the basic course for ten years. Many of his former pupils have themselves become teachers, spreading his teaching methods and his belief in the economy of creative means throughout the world. At last his art is finding the recognition it deserves. Those he has taught are now applying its principles, and his fame echoes back from America to the country of his origin. The world-wide influence of Josef Albers is the most impressive testimony to the dissemination of the idea which was the Bauhaus.

CONCLUSION

The Bauhaus has changed our environment by transforming and re-forming the *Wesen und Gestalt der Dinge um uns* (Nature and Shape of Things Around Us), to quote the title of a book by Wilhelm Wagenfeld, a former Bauhaus student. The effects of this transformation are now such a normal and accepted part of our environment that it is difficult to imagine anything else. Our houses, furniture, offices, and industrial equipment all owe their clean, uncluttered, elegant forms to the creative ideas that originated in the Bauhaus. While it would be wrong to say that without the Bauhaus these changes would not have occurred, it would be equally incorrect to maintain that the idea realized by Gropius was part of the *Zeitgeist* and would have asserted itself without him. The Bauhaus embodied the intuition of a creative genius who, inspired by the spirit of medieval humanism, insisted that the teaching of the true artist must combine a deep and thorough technical training with a wide liberal education. Although the first Bauhaus teachers were painters, the transformation of man's environment went far beyond the sphere of painting to encompass every form of creative design: architecture, interior decoration, furniture design, textiles, industrial design, advertising, typography, exhibition planning, the cinema, theatre, dance, education, and so on. To the question 'Where is the Bauhaus today?', one can truly answer, 'It is all around us'.

However, the Bauhaus cannot be found everywhere in its pure form. Others took over the features, materials, and methods developed at the Bauhaus but, instead of the expected recipe book, they found an empty shell which, lacking imagination, they were incapable of filling with a new spirit. Every new idea is beset by this danger: as soon as it becomes the accepted style of a period, it is diluted and devalued by men of lesser talent. This gradual loss of the original meaning followed by decline is a normal historical process of wear and tear. Examples of this phenomenon can be seen in the dull, monotonous products of our mass-produced contemporary architecture, which look like the misbegotten step-children of the Bauhaus idea. The painters contributed to the change in our environment by regenerating and revitalizing the visual arts, by re-examining the fundamentals of aesthetics, and by giving impetus to the reappraisal of the meaning of art. The profound creative insights formulated by Klee and Kandinsky in their lectures have become part of our common artistic culture. The teaching methods evolved for the basic course by both Itten and Albers have spread far and wide—in fact, one may well ask if there is any place left where they are not applied. In Germany, at any rate, they have been in general use since 1945.

The painters played a vital part in the Bauhaus; in fact, it would be unthinkable without thcm. But, although they strongly influenced the shaping of its policy, they were by no means the only influence, and the overriding image of the Bauhaus is one of collaboration on a communal task in all its manifold aspects. A book about the Bauhaus painters can only attempt to deal with one particular aspect, and must of necessity remain one-sided. Each of the chapters dealing with one painter spotlights only a single facet of the whole, leaving the rest in semi-darkness. A more thorough and comprehensive study is outside the scope of this work, but the method used—lifting out individual aspects for close examination—requires us, at the conclusion, to relate these individual features to the general context. We must, therefore, mention those personalities who could not be considered on account of thematic limitations, for example, students, and teachers of other subjects.

The Bauhaus pottery was housed in Dornburg Castle on the river Saale near Weimar. The teacher in charge was the sculptor *Gerhard Marcks*, born in 1889 in Berlin, where he studied under August Gaul, Georg Kolbe, and Richard Scheibe. He had known Gropius since before World War I and was one of the first masters to be appointed by the Bauhaus. Marcks did not move with the Bauhaus to Dessau but accepted a teaching appointment at the Burg Giebichenstein art school at Halle, of which he later became head. He was dismissed in 1933 and branded 'decadent' by the Nazis. For the duration of the Nazi regime, he lived in retirement at Arenshoop on the Baltic. From 1946 to 1950, he held a professorship at the art school of the province of Hanover. In 1950, Marcks moved to Cologne, where he still lives.

Gertrud Grunow was appointed to the Bauhaus on Itten's recommendation. She was born in Berlin in 1880. In her classes and in her personal advice to students, she provided a philosophic framework for the synaesthetic ideas which determined the thought and work of many Bauhaus artists. She taught that there is a basic harmony which has its origin in the fundamental unity of the forces of nature, and which, in the last resort, governs all the different appearances of physical reality, which are transmitted to our observation and consciousness through the different organs of sensory perception. Gertrud Grunow did not go to Dessau. She pursued her further research and studies in comparative seclusion, surrounded by a small circle of friends. She died at Leverkusen in 1944.

Marcel Breuer, Hinnerk Scheper, Joost Schmidt, and Gunta Stölzl belonged to the generation of young masters at the Dessau Bauhaus. *Marcel Breuer* is one of the most significant architects and furniture designers of this century. He was born in 1902 at Pécs in Hungary, and his first ambition was to become a sculptor. On entering the Bauhaus in 1920, however, he discovered cabinet-making as his true vocation. As early as 1921, he began to make a name for himself with his unusual furniture designs. In 1925, he was placed in charge of the carpentry and furniture workshop at the Dessau Bauhaus. From 1928 to 1931, he lived mainly in Berlin, where he worked a great deal with Gropius. In 1935, he moved to London, and in 1937 to Cambridge, Massachusetts, having been appointed a professor at Harvard University. From 1937 to 1941, he worked with Gropius as an architect, and in 1946 he set up in private architectural practice in New York, New York and New Canaan, Connecticut.

Hinnerk Scheper pioneered the practice of contemporary wall decoration consistent with the new spatial relationships created by modern architecture. Scheper was born in 1897 at Badbergen near Osnabrück. Before joining the Bauhaus as a student in 1919, he had undergone thorough training as a mural painter and had studied at the School of Arts and Crafts and at the Art Academy in Düsseldorf. At the Bauhaus, he made an intensive study of the requirements and problems connected with giving walls a neat, clear appearance in a modern setting. He obtained his master's diploma in 1922 and, until 1925, continued his studies on his own and did free-lance work. By the time he was appointed to his teaching post at Dessau he was recognized as a leading authority in his field. He took over the department of mural painting and remained at the Bauhaus until it was closed in Berlin in 1933. From 1928 to 1931, he received temporary leave of absence to enable him to work in Moscow as a specialist consultant on architectural design in relation to colour. On his return, he took on the artistic design of Bauhaus wallpapers, in addition to his other duties. During the Nazi era, he managed to earn his living, though under difficult conditions, by doing free-lance work. In 1945, the Berlin City Council appointed him Curator, and in 1953 he was promoted to the position of State Curator of the West Berlin district. He died in 1957.

Joost Schmidt worked in many fields, particularly in sculpture, advertising design, typography, and exhibition architecture. He was born in 1893 at Wunstorf in Lower Saxony, and he spent his early years at Hamelin. From 1910 to 1914, he studied painting at the Weimar School of Arts and Crafts. During World War I, he served in the infantry and was taken prisoner by the Americans. On his release from the POW camp in 1919, he returned to Weimar and continued his studies at the Bauhaus. He worked mainly in the sculpture workshop and in the printing shop. He obtained a diploma in sculpture and in 1926 was offered a teaching post at the Dessau Bauhaus, where he took over the sculpture class. In 1928, after Bayer's departure, Schmidt was also placed in charge of the printing shop. When the Bauhaus had to leave Dessau, he took up appointments with Hugo Häring and the Reimann School in Berlin, until he was forbidden to work by order of the Nazi government. From 1938 to 1944, he wrote a *Geschichte der Perspektive* (History of Perspective), but in 1944, he was again called up to the army. In 1945, he returned to Berlin, where he became a professor at the College of Visual Arts and conducted the basic course for architects. He died in Nuremberg in 1948.

Gunta Stölzl was born in Munich in 1897. She studied at the Munich School of Arts and Crafts 1914–19, and became a student at the Bauhaus in 1919. After obtaining her weaving diploma, she became technical supervisor of the weaving department under Muche's artistic direction. After Muche's departure in 1927, she was appointed as his successor and took control of the whole department. She left the Bauhaus in 1931 to devote herself to her own weaving shop in Zürich. She has helped run a weaving workshop at Herrliberg near Zürich since 1924.

The architect *Hans Wittwer,* born in Basle in 1894, joined the Bauhaus in 1927, at the same time as Hannes Meyer. In 1928, Meyer—now head of the Dessau Bauhaus—offered him a senior post, and Wittwer became chief designer. His lectures dealt with building problems and questions of acoustics, light, and heating techniques. In 1929, he was appointed to the Burg Giebichenstein art school. In 1934, he returned to Basle, where he died in 1952.

The architect and twon planner *Ludwig Hilberseimer,* born in 1885 at Karlsruhe, became head of the Bauhaus building department in 1929. He remained at the Bauhaus until its closure in 1933. He lived in Berlin until 1938, when he emigrated to the United States. He was appointed professor of town planning in the architecture department of the Illinois Institute of Technology in Chicago.

Alfred Arndt, born at Königsberg in 1898, studied at the Königsberg Art Academy. From 1921 to 1926, he continued his studies at the Bauhaus, specializing in mural painting and architecture. He set up an architectural practice at Probstzella in Thuringia, but returned to the Dessau Bauhaus as a teacher in 1929. Until 1931, he was in charge of the furniture workshop, and while Scheper was on his long leave of absence, Arndt also looked after the mural painting workshop. When the Dessau Bauhaus was wound up in 1932, he left to return to Probstzella. In 1948, he moved to Darmstadt, where he now lives.

The Dutchman *Mart Stam,* born at Purmerend in 1899, was a guest lecturer at the Bauhaus in 1928–29. He lectured on elementary building techniques and town planning. Stam derived his philosophy from the functionalism of the Dutch *De Stijl* group. At the time of his connection with the Bauhaus he was a widely-known and respected architect, town planner, and estate developer, who had distinguished himself by his original architectural designs. He spent most of 1929–35 in Russia, and 1935–48 in Amsterdam, where he became Director of the Teaching Institute of the Art Industry in 1939. In 1948, he accepted an appointment as Director of the Dresden Academy of Art, and in 1950, Director of the Academy of Art in Berlin-Weissensee. He returned to Amsterdam in 1953.

Anton Brenner, born in Vienna in 1896, was a pupil of Behrens and Holzmeister. He directed the architectural studios at the Bauhaus from the spring of 1929 to the summer of 1930. He died in Vienna in 1957.

Alcar Rudelt, born in Leipzig in 1900, trained as an architectural engineer in Berlin. From the autumn of 1928 to the spring of 1933, he taught mathematics, structural science, steel and concrete building techniques, and heating and ventilation. After the closure of the Bauhaus, he moved to Hanover.

The Norwegian *Edvard Heiberg,* who was born in Oslo 1897, taught in the architecture department during the first half of 1920. He went to Moscow with Meyer. From 1932, he worked on housing-estate design in Copenhagen. He was imprisoned in a concentration camp during the war, and he died in Copenhagen in 1958.

Walter Peterhans was in charge of the Bauhaus photographic department founded in 1929, and remained there until 1933. He was born in Frankfurt-am-Main in 1897. He spent his childhood days in Dresden and studied at the Munich Technical High School. He went on to study mathematics, philosophy, and art history at Göttingen University and at the State Academy of the Graphic Arts and the Book Industry in Leipzig. Moholy-Nagy's efforts in the field of photography had aroused interest in this new artistic discipline and had inspired the introduction of a course in photography at the Bauhaus. Peterhans treated the subject in depth and made photography the equal of the traditional branches of art. After the dissolution of the Bauhaus, he remained in Berlin until 1937. He emigrated to the United States in 1938 and became a professor at the Illinois Institute of Technology in Chicago, where he taught the elementary art courses and also art history. He has published several treatises on photographic problems. He died at Stetten, near Stuttgart, in 1960.

Otti Berger, who was born at Vörösmart, Hungary, in 1898, joined the Bauhaus weaving department in 1927. After the departure of Gunta Stölzl, she was in charge of the weaving workshop for a short time. Later, she lived in Berlin, where she worked with a number of important German and foreign textile firms. She perished in a concentration camp in 1942.

Karla Grosch, who was born in Weimar in 1904, taught gymnastics and was a dancer at the Bauhaus Theatre. She drowned at Tel Aviv in 1933.

The Hungarian *Ernst Kállai,* who was born in 1890 at Szakaházá, spent a short period in America before 1914. He came to Germany in 1920. In 1928–29, he edited the Bauhaus magazine. From 1935, he lived in Budapest, where he became a professor at the School of Arts and Crafts in 1946. He died in 1954.

Walter Gropius, the founder of the Bauhaus and its first Director, returned to Berlin after his resignation from the Bauhaus, and worked there as an architect. In 1929, he received an honorary doctor's degree in engineering from the Hanover College of Technology. He emigrated to England in 1934 and worked with Maxwell Fry in London. In 1937, he was invited to join the Graduate School of Design, Harvard University, Cambridge, Massachusetts. From 1938 to 1952, he was head of its Department of Architecture. He designed a large number of buildings in the United States, at first in partnership with Marcel Breuer. In 1946, he founded the Architects' Collaborative, a co-operative undertaking which, under his leadership, obtained important commissions in a number of countries. Argan's monograph covering the period 1906–56 (*Gropius und das Bauhaus* [Gropius and the Bauhaus], pp. 119 ff.) gives an extensive list of the buildings erected from Gropius' designs in Germany, Sweden, the Soviet Union, South America, Great Britain, the United States,

China, Iraq, and Greece. In recent years, he has again accepted commissions for his native Berlin.

Hannes Meyer, who was born at Basle in 1889, succeeded Gropius as Director of the Bauhaus. He studied at the Basle School of Arts and Crafts from 1905 to 1909, and, from then until 1912, at the School of Arts and Crafts in Berlin. This was followed by a year of study in England. In 1919, Meyer started a private architectural practice in Basle. By that time, he had gained considerable experience, particularly in estate planning, while working on municipal projects at Munich, Essen, and Lausanne. From 1926, he worked in partnership with Hans Wittwer. During his period of office as Bauhaus Director, new staff appointments were mostly of architects. Following his dismissal from the Bauhaus, Meyer accepted a professorship at the Moscow College of Architecture. From 1936 to 1939, he worked on urban planning in Geneva. In 1939, he was appointed Direktor of the 'Instituto de Urbanismo y Planificación' in Mexico, where he remained for ten years. From his return to Switzerland in 1949 until his death in 1954, he lived at Crocifisso di Savosa-Lugano, in the Ticino.

The third and last Bauhaus Director, *Ludwig Mies van der Rohe,* was born at Aachen in 1886 and moved to Berlin in 1905. Until 1907, he worked as an apprentice in the office of the architect Bruno Paul, and from 1908 to 1911, he was Peter Behrens' assistant. He set up his own Berlin practice in 1912. From 1914 to 1918 he served in the army. On his return, he developed his own, modern architectural style, based on engineering principles. It was a bold and powerful style which has left its imprint on the urban civilization of our time in every country of the world. Mies van der Rohe was a member of the 'November Group' founded in Berlin after the war. In 1925, together with nine other architects, he founded an association called 'Der Ring'. In 1926, following his appointment as Vice-Chairman of the German Werkbund, he was commissioned to organize the construction of the Weissenhof estate at Stuttgart. He maintained his architectural practice in Berlin side by side with his activities at the Bauhaus; he finally gave up his practice in 1937, when he made his first trip to the United States. The following year, he emigrated to the United States and settled in Chicago. In that same year, he became Director of the Architecture Department of the Armour Institute, which was renamed in 1940 the Illinois Institute of Technology. Since 1945, many impressive major building projects have been completed from his designs, in the United States and later in Germany (for example, the administration building of the Krupp works in Essen). He also did some work for postwar Berlin, designing the projected Exhibition Hall of Twentieth-Century Art. Mies van der Rohe is one of the most important architects of our time, and his name ranks with those of Gropius, Le Corbusier, and Frank Lloyd Wright.

Of the many students at Weimar and Dessau who later became artists, there is room to mention only a few:

Mordecai Ardon (formerly *Bronstein*), born at Tuchow, Poland, in 1896, studied with Klee, Kandinsky, and Itten and later taught at Itten's art school in Berlin. He emigrated to Palestine in 1933 and taught at the Bezalel Art School in Jerusalem, becoming director of the school in 1940. In 1952, he became art adviser to the Israeli Ministry of Education. After attaining a local reputation, he emerged in the 1950's as an important painter, with exhibitions in European and American museums and galleries. He is a remarkable colourist who combines formal brilliance with a powerful oneiric fantasy. Monumental triptychs can be seen at the Amsterdam Stedelijk, and his *Missa Dura* at the Tate Gallery in London is of special interest.

Max Bill was born at Winterthur, Switzerland, in 1908, and studied at Dessau. Bill belongs to the exponents of concrete art. In 1944, he organized the international exhibition 'Concrete Art' at the Basle Kunsthalle. As Director of the Hochschule für Gestaltung (College of Design) at Ulm from 1951 to 1956, he made a brave attempt to translate the basic stylistic philosophy of the Bauhaus into the idiom of postwar Germany, but finally had to admit that this was impossible.

> I often find myself in the position of having to explain that the Bauhaus laid the foundations for many new possibilities which, at the time, it was not in a position to develop to their full potential. I am of the opinion that many opportunities not developed at that time remain undeveloped still. Or, what is worse, they are being developed in a manner which is a complete misinterpretation of the original intentions. The high hopes I had when the Hochschule für Gestaltung was founded at Ulm, have, unfortunately, not been realized so far. Nor can I see anywhere else a real development of the Bauhaus idea as a whole. All one can find is partial features taken out of context, and false interpretations which stand in the way of the true development of the original ideas. In spite of all these false starts, it remains my firm conviction that it is necessary to overcome the shallow commercialization of the "design" business and the present aimlessness in the shaping of our environment; the only real chance lies in adapting the basic principles of the Bauhaus to the present time, and in reviving a true, responsible outlook in design. (*Bauhaus Catalogue*, Frankfurt, 1964, pp. 129 ff.)

Paul Citroen, born in Berlin in 1896, the son of Dutch parents, studied at the Bauhaus under Klee and Kandinsky. He created the large-scale 'townscape' photomontages, which were completely new at the time. He now lives in Amsterdam. The *Bauhaus Catalogue*, published at Frankfurt in 1964, contains a lively description by him of 'Mazdaznan at the Bauhaus'. (*Bauhaus Catalogue*, Frankfurt, 1964, pp. 29 ff.)

Werner Gilles, born at Rheydt in the Rhineland in 1894, studied at Weimar. His 'Meditations', filled with southern landscapes and ancient mythology, were inspired by Klee and Feininger. The evening of his life and his art were dominated by the landscape of Ischia. He died in 1961.

Wilhelm Imkamp, born at Münster in Westphalia in 1906, studied at the Dessau Bauhaus under Kandinsky and Klee. He now works at Stuttgart as an abstract painter.

Ida Kerkovius, born at Riga in 1897, was a friend of Itten's and belonged to the Hölzl circle at Stuttgart, which moulded her artistic outlook. She studied at the Weimar Bauhaus for a few terms. She had already developed her own individual style—a forceful, colourful Expressionism—to which she has remained faithful to this day. At the Bauhaus, she spent most of her time in the weaving workshop and made a number of wall hangings. She now lives in Stuttgart.

The painter *Fritz Kuhr*, born in 1895 at Liège, is at present a professor in the pedagogic department of the Hochschule für Bildende Künste (College of Visual Art) in Berlin. It was he who, as a student, made a moving impromptu speech when Gropius announced his resignation, in which he tried to dissuade the Director from leaving the Bauhaus.

Lucia Moholy-Nagy was also a Bauhaus student. Like her husband Laszlo, she was engaged in artistic and experimental photography. She now lives in Switzerland.

Helene Nonne-Schmidt, wife of the Bauhaus teacher Joost Schmidt, studied under Klee and worked mostly in the weaving department. She lives in Darmstadt.

Richard Oelze, born at Magdeburg in 1900, studied at the Bauhaus from 1921 to 1926. He made his first contact with the Surrealists during a stay in Paris in 1932. It was only later that the individuality of his style gained recognition in Germany. He only became known in artistic circles when his pictures were shown at the *Dokumenta II* at Kassel in 1955. Since that year, he has had several one-man shows. He now lives in retirement at Posteholz, near Hamelin.

Max Pfeiffer-Watenphul and *Erich Pfeiffer-Belli* were Bauhaus students. The latter became a writer and has published a spirited biography of Paul Klee, largely based on his own reminiscences. (Pfeiffer-Belli, *Klee*, Kindler's Bildbiographien, Munich, 1964.)

Alexander Schawinski, nicknamed Xanti, was a pupil of Kandinsky's. He was a member of the Bauhaus band, and he made stage designs for the Bauhaus Theatre. He turned to exhibition design and advertising, where he distinguished himself by powerful and original layouts often containing Surrealist elements. In 1926, the Zwickau Municipal Theatre appointed him as stage designer. He now lives in New York, where he works as a graphic artist.

The painter *Lou Scheper-Berkenkamp,* Hinnerk Scheper's wife, was born at Wesel in 1901. She now lives in Berlin. Her playfully imaginative, finely drawn landscapes can often be seen at exhibitions.

Hans Thiemann, born in 1910 at Langendreer, near Bochum, is now a painter and stage designer living in Berlin. From 1929 to 1933, he studied under Klee and Kandinsky. His compositions are influenced by Magic Realism and by Surrealism.

The abstract painter *Fritz Winter,* born in 1905 at Altenbögge, studied under Schlemmer, Kandinsky, and Klee from 1927 to 1930. One of Germany's most important exponents of nonobjective painting, he now lives at Diessen on Ammersee.

The above are only a few names which serve to illustrate the range and talent of many artists who where at the Bauhaus.

The Bauhaus sent forth its apostles. At Weimar and Dessau, artists and craftsmen came together, speaking many tongues yet understanding each other. They came from many countries and were dispersed to all corners of the earth. In this way, the idea underlying the Bauhaus has become an integral part of our civilization.

A resurrection of the Bauhaus itself is not now possible, since it was the sum total of the active collaboration of certain outstanding personalities, including the painters, against the background of a spiritual climate and other imponderables determined by specific circumstances of history.

There have been attempts to reconstruct it; for example, the New Bauhaus started by Moholy-Nagy in Chicago; the *Mühely*—the so-called Budapest Bauhaus—founded in 1929; and, finally, Max Bill's endeavours to revive the Bauhaus idea in the Hochschule für Gestaltung at Ulm. But all these attempts were doomed to failure. Their results turned out to be totally different from what had been intended or expected. It must be accepted that different personalities and different periods produce their distinctive means of expression.

There is an imperceptible change in accepted standards and ideals as time marches on. After a period of fifty years, the Bauhaus has already found its place in history, and the painters who taught at the Bauhaus have become the classic masters of twentieth-century art.

BIOGRAPHICAL NOTES

Josef Albers

Born 1888 at Bottrop, Westphalia. Studied at Royal Academy of Art in Berlin, 1913–15, then in Essen and Munich. Student at Weimar Bauhaus, 1920—23. Master at Dessau Bauhaus, mainly in charge of basic course, 1925–33. Professor at Black Mountain College, North Carolina, 1933–49. Professor at Yale University, 1950–59. Now working as independent artist in New Haven, Connecticut.

Herbert Bayer

Born 1900 at Haag, Austria. Military service, 1917–19, followed by architecture and craft studies at Linz. Student at Weimar Bauhaus, 1921–23. Master at Dessau Bauhaus, 1925–28. Main subjects taught: typography, advertising design. In Berlin, 1928–38, working as advertising and exhibition designer and typographer. Artistic consultant to Wanamaker's Department Store and J. Walter Thompson Advertising Agency, New York, 1938–46. Since 1946, has lived in Aspen, Colorado.

Lyonel Feininger

Born 1871 in New York. Student at Hamburg School of Arts and Crafts, 1887. Student at Berlin Academy, 1888–91. First caricatures and illustrations. Paris, 1906, meets artists of the Dôme circle. First paintings, 1907. Marriage to Julia Berg, 1908. Meets Cubists in Paris, 1911. Mostly in Berlin, 1912–19. Exhibits in First German Autumn Salon in Berlin, together with Blaue Reiter artists, 1913. Master at Bauhaus, 1919–33: in charge of printing workshop at Weimar; allowed to give up teaching duties on moving to Dessau. Berlin, 1933–36. Visit to New York, 1936; decision not to return to Germany. Emigration to United States, 1937. New York, 1938–56. First important Feininger exhibition at the Museum of Modern Art, 1944. Died in New York, 1956.

Johannes Itten

Born 1888 at Südern-Linden, Switzerland. Student at teachers training college, Berlin, 1904–8; first attempts at painting. Student at Ecole des Beaux Arts, Geneva, 1909–10. Student at Stuttgart Academy of Art under Hölzel, 1913–16. Meets Schlemmer and Baumeister. First non-figurative paintings, 1915. Vienna, 1916–19; first Itten school. Master at Weimar Bauhaus, 1919–23, mainly as head of basic course. Herrliberg, Switzerland, 1923–26. Foundation and direction of own school in Berlin, 1926–31. Teacher at Krefeld School of Textile Design, 1932. Director of same school, 1936. Amsterdam, 1938. Later in the same year, director of the School of Applied Arts in Zurich. Became director of College of Textile Design, Zurich, 1943; organized foundation of Rietberg Museum, under his direction. Until his death in 1967, worked as an artist in Zurich.

Wassily Kandinsky

Born 1866 in Moscow. Studied law and economics in Odessa and Moscow. Ethnographic research expedition to Vologda province, 1889. Law examinations, 1893. Move to Munich, 1896; study of painting at the Azbé school and at the Academy of Art under Franz von Stuck. Chairman of Phalanx, Munich artists' association, 1901. Journeys to Holland, Tunisia, Italy, 1904. Dresden, 1905. Sèvres, near Paris, 1906–7. Return to Munich, 1908. Beginning of friendship with Marianne von Werefkin and Alexei Jawlensky. First abstract water-colour, 1910. Meets Marc, Klee, Arp, Macke, 1910; foundation and first show of the Blaue Reiter. Publication of Concerning the Spiritual in Art and Blaue Reiter Almanach. Publication of autobiographical Rückblicke (Backward Glances) by Sturm publishing house, 1913. At outbreak of war, 1914, return to Moscow. Three months in Stockholm, 1916. Trip to Finland, 1917; same year, marriage to Nina von Andreewsky. Member of the Department of Art of the Commissariat for Popular Education, 1918. Professor at Academy of Art. Founds Museum of Painting Culture, 1919, and reorganizes twenty-two Russian provincial museums. Professor at Moscow University, 1920. End of 1921, arrival in Berlin. Master at Bauhaus, 1922–33. Publication of Point and Line to Plane, 1926. German citizenship, 1928. Move to Berlin with Bauhaus, 1933. Same year, emigration to France. Confiscation of 57 works branded 'decadent' by Nazi regime, 1937. French citizenship, 1939. Died at Neuilly-sur-Seine, 1944.

Paul Klee

Born 1879 at Münchenbuchsee, near Berne. Matriculation at Berne grammar school, 1898. Studies under Knirr at Munich Art College and under Stuck at Munich Academy of Art, 1898–1901. Berne, 1902–6. Marriage to Lily Stumpf in Munich, 1906. First comprehensive exhibition, 1911, at Thannhauser Gallery, Munich. Meets Kandinsky, Marc, Macke, Kubin, Jawlensky, and Marianne von Werefkin. Takes part in Blaue Reiter exhibition, 1912. Meets Delaunay in Paris. Journey to Kairouan and Tunis with Macke and Moilliet, 1914. Military service, 1916–18. Master at Bauhaus, 1921–31. Publication of Pedagogical Sketchbook, 1925. Winter 1928—29, visit to Egypt. Professor at Düsseldorf Art Academy, 1931–33. Return to Berlin, 1933. Confiscation of 102 works branded 'decadent' by Nazi regime, 1937. First signs of illness, 1935. Died at Muralto, near Locarno, 1940.

Laszlo Moholy-Nagy

Born 1895 at Bácsborsòd, Hungary. Studied law in Budapest. Military service, 1915–18. First paintings during convalescence from war wound. Degree in law, Budapest, 1918. In Berlin as painter and author of articles on art, 1920–23. Meets

El Lissitzky in Düsseldorf, 1921; first abstract paintings, which are exhibited in Sturm Gallery, Berlin. Master at Bauhaus in Weimar and Dessau, 1923–28, in charge of basic course and metal-work course. Publication of *Malerei, Photographie, Film*, 1925. Move to Berlin, 1928. London, 1935–37. Chicago, 1937–46; foundation of The New Bauhaus. Died in Chicago, 1946.

Georg Muche

Born 1895 at Querfurt. Studied art in Munich and Berlin, 1913–15. Director of Sturm art school, Berlin, 1917–20. Exhibitions at Sturm Gallery. Master at Weimar and Dessau Bauhaus, in charge of textile workshop, 1920–27. Design and erection of an experimental house at Weimar, 1923. Study trip to United States, 1924. Teacher at Itten school, Berlin, 1927–31. Professor at State Academy of Art, Breslau, 1931–33. Berlin, 1933–38. Confiscation of 13 works declared 'decadent' by Nazi regime, 1937. Publication of book *Buon Fresco* (letters from Italy concerning the craft and style of genuine fresco painting), 1938. Foundation and direction of a master class in textile art at Krefeld School of Textile Design. At Dr Kurt Herbert's *Institut für Malstoffkunde* (Institute for Study of Paint Materials) in Wuppertal, 1942, together with Schlemmer and Baumeister. Move to Lindau on the Bodensee, 1960.

Oskar Schlemmer

Born 1888 at Stuttgart. Student at Stuttgart Academy of Art under Hölzel, 1909–14 and 1918–19. Friendship with Baumeister, Meyer-Amden, and Itten. Military service, 1914–18. First performance of completed part of Triadic Ballet, 1916. Master at Weimar and Dessau Bauhaus, 1920–29, mainly in charge of theatre workshop. Mural painting in entrance hall of workshop building of Weimar Bauhaus, 1923. Mural paintings for Folkwang Museum, Essen, 1928. Professor at State Academy of Art, Breslau, 1929–32. Professor at Berlin Academy, 1932–33. Dismissed by Nazis, 1933. At Eichberg in South Baden, 1935–37. At Sehringen, near Badenweiler, 1937—43. At Dr Kurt Herbert's *Institut für Malstoffkunde* in Wuppertal, 1942, together with Muche and Baumeister. Died at Baden-Baden, 1943.

Lothar Schreyer

Born 1886 at Blasewitz, near Dresden. Studied art history and law at Heidelberg, Berlin, and Leipzig. Passed law examinations. Producer at Deutsches Schauspielhaus (German Theatre), Hamburg. Contributor to and, at times, editor of the Sturm magazine, 1916–28. Founder and director of the Sturm Theatre, 1916–20. Return to Hamburg and foundation of Kampf Theatre. Teacher at Bauhaus, 1920–23. Numerous publications. Poems and works on Christian art. Lived in Hamburg until his death in 1966.

BIBLIOGRAPHY

A comprehensive bibliography on the Bauhaus is contained in Wingler's documentary work *Das Bauhaus,* in the list below. Therefore, with a few exceptions, this bibliography includes mainly publications mentioned in the text.

GROPIUS AND THE BAUHAUS

Argan, Giulio Carlo. *Gropius und das Bauhaus.* Rowohlt's German Encyclopedia, No. 149. Reinbeck bei Hamburg: 1962.

Bauhaus: Zeitschrift für Bau und Gestaltung (Bauhaus: Building and Construction Publication). Dessau: 1926, 1928.

Bayer, Herbert, Gropius, Walter, and Gropius, Ise. *Bauhaus 1919–1928.* Newton Centre, Mass.: Charles T. Branford, 1959.

Die Bauhaus-Mappen. Neue Europäische Graphik 1921–23 (The Bauhaus Portfolio. New European Graphics 1921–23), ed. Heinz Peters. New York: George Wittenborn, Inc., 1957.

Giedion, Siegfried. *Walter Gropius: Mensch und Werk.* Stuttgart: 1954. Published as *Walter Gropius: Work and Teamwork.* New York: Reinhold, 1954.

Naumann, Friedrich. *Deutsche Gewerbekunst* (German Applied Arts). Berlin: 1908.

Staatliches Bauhaus Weimar 1919–1923. Munich, Weimar: 1923.

Wagenfeld, Wilhelm. *Wesen und Gestalt der Dinge um uns* (The Nature and Shape of Things Around Us). Potsdam: 1948.

Wingler, Hans M. *Das Bauhaus 1919–1933: Weimar-Dessau-Berlin.* Bramsche: 1962.

Catalogues

Arbeiten aus der graphischen Druckerei des Staatlichen Bauhauses 1919–1925 (Works from the Graphic Press of the Bauhaus 1919–1925). Exhibition held in Darmstadt, March–May, 1963.

Bauhaus: Idee-Form-Zweck-Zeit-Dokumente und Äusserungen (Bauhaus: Idea, Form, Goal, Era, Documents and Proclamations). Exhibition held in Frankfurt, Göppinger Gallery, February–March, 1964.

Die Maler am Bauhaus (Painters of the Bauhaus). Edited and with an introduction by Ludwig Grote. Munich: 1950.

Painters of the Bauhaus. Assembled and with an introduction by Will Grohmann. Exhibition held in London, Marlborough Fine Art Ltd., March–April, 1962.

JOSEF ALBERS

Albers, Josef. *Interaction of Color.* New Haven, Conn.: Yale University Press. 1963.

———. 'Selbstbericht' (Personal Account), *Die Zeit ohne Eigenschaften: Eine Bilanz der zwanziger Jahre* (The Time Without Characteristics: A Balance Sheet of the Twenties), ed. Leonhard Reinisch. Stuttgart: 1961.

———. 'Werklicher Formunterricht' (Practical Instruction in the Making of Forms), *Bauhaus,* Vol. II, No. 2/3, Dessau: 1928.

———, and Lohse, Richard P, 'City 1928', *Zürcher Kunstgesellschaft, Jahresbericht* (Zürich Society of Art, Annual Report), 1960.

Bucher, François. *Josef Albers: Trotz der Geraden.* Includes a lengthy bibliography. Bern: 1961. Published as *Josef Albers: Despite Straight Lines—Analysis of His Graphic Constructions.* New Haven, Conn.: Yale University Press, 1961.

Catalogue

Josef Albers. Exhibition held in Raleigh, N. C., Museum of Art, February–March, 1962.

HERBERT BAYER

Bayer, Herbert. 'Typographie und Werbsachengestaltung' (Typography and the Layout of Publicity Material), *Bauhaus,* Vol. II, No. 1, Dessau, 1928.

Catalogue

Herbert Bayer. Exhibition held at Duisburg, Municipal Art Museum, February–March, 1962.

LYONEL FEININGER

Hess, Hans (ed.). *Lyonel Feininger.* Compiled by Annemarie Heynig. Includes catalogue of works and complete bibliography. Stuttgart: 1959. Published as *Lyonel Feininger.* New York: Harry N. Abrams, Inc. 1961.

JOHANNES ITTEN

Itten, Johannes. *Kunst der Farbe: Subjektives Erleben und objektives Erkennen als Wege zur Kunst.* Ravensburg: 1961. Published as *The Art of Color: Subjective Experience and Objective Understanding as the Path to Art.* New York: Reinhold, 1961.

———. *Mein Vorkurs am Bauhaus: Gestaltungs- und Formenlehre.* Ravensburg: 1963. Published as *Design and Form: The Basic Course at the Bauhaus.* New York: Reinhold, 1964.

———. *Tagebuch: Beitrag zu einem Kontrapunkt der bildenden Kunst* (Diary: Toward a Counterpoint to Visual Art). Berlin: 1930.

Tietze-Conrat, Erika. 'Johannes Itten: Über das Beschreiben von Bildern' ('Johannes Itten: On His Writings About Pictures'), *Die bildenden Künste* (The Visual Art), Vol. II, Vienna, 1919.

Catalogues

Johannes Itten. Amsterdam Stedelijk Museum Catalogue No. 109, April–May, 1957.

Johannes Itten. Exhibition held in Zurich, Art Museum, April–May, 1964.

WASSILY KANDINSKY

Brisch, Klaus. *Wassily Kandinsky 1866–1944: Untersuchungen zur Entstehung der gegenstandslosen Malerei an seinem Werk von 1900–21*

(Investigations Into the Rise of Non-Objective Painting in His Work from 1900–21). Dissertation (typescript). Bonn: 1955.

Grohmann, Will. *Wassily Kandinsky: Leben und Werk.* Includes a list of works, a list of exhibitions, and a complete bibliography. Cologne: 1958. Published as *Kandinsky.* New York: Harry N. Abrams, 1958.

Kandinsky, Wassily. 'Der gelbe Klang, eine Bühnenkomposition' (The Yellow Sound, a Stage Composition), *Der Blaue Reiter,* Munich, 1912.

———. *Kandinsky Album: Rückblicke 1901–13* (Retrospective 1901–13), New edition, with introduction by Ludwig Grote. Baden-Baden: 1955.

———. *Punkt und Linie zu Fläche: Beitrag zu einer Analyse der malerischen Elemente,* Bauhaus Books, No. 9. Munich: 1926. New edition, with an introduction by Max Bill. Berne: 1955. Published as *Point and Line to Plane: Contribution to the Analysis of Pictorial Elements.* New York: Solomon R. Guggenheim Museum, 1948.

———. *Über das Geistige in der Kunst, insbesondere der Malerei.* Munich: 1912. New edition, with an introduction by Max Bill. Berne: 1952. Published as *Concerning the Spiritual in Art, and Painting in Particular.* New York: George Wittenborn, Inc., 1964.

Klee, Paul. *Kandinsky.* In the catalogue of the Jubilee Exhibition on Kandinsky's sixtieth birthday, Dresden, 1926.

Lassaigne, Jacques. *Kandinsky.* Cleveland and New York: World Publishing Co. (Skira Art Books), 1964.

Catalogue

Vasily Kandinsky 1866–1944. Exhibition held in New York, Solomon R. Guggenheim Museum, 1962.

PAUL KLEE

Baumeister, Willi. *Das Unbekannte in der Kunst* (The Unknown in Art). Stuttgart: 1947.

Grohmann, Will. *Paul Klee.* Includes catalogue of the group, chronological catalogue, and complete bibliography. Stuttgart: 1954. Published as *Paul Klee.* New York: Harry N. Abrams, 1967.

Grohmann, Will. *Paul Klee: Handzeichnungen* (Paul Klee: Drawings). Cologne: 1959.

Grote, Ludwig (ed.). *Erinnerungen an Paul Klee* (Memories of Paul Klee). Munich: 1959.

Klee, Felix. *Paul Klee: Leben und Werk in Dokumenten, ausgewählt aus den nachgelassenen Aufzeichnungen und den unveröffentlichten Briefen* (Paul Klee: Life and Work in Documents Chosen from the Unpublished Drawings and Letters). Zürich: 1960.

Klee, Paul. *Das bildnerische Denken: Schriften zur Form- und Gestaltungslehre* (Pictorial Thinking: Writings on a Theory of Form and Representation), ed. Jürg Spiller. Basel, Stuttgart: 1957.

———. *Pädagogisches Skizzenbuch.* Bauhaus Books, No. 2. Munich: 1925. New edition, Mainz, Berlin: 1965. Published as *Pedagogical Sketchbook.* New York: Frederick A. Praeger, 1953.

———. *Schöpferische Konfession: Tribüne der Kunst und Zeit* (Artistic Confessions: Tribunal of Art and Time), ed. Kasimir Edschmidt. Berlin: 1920.

———. *Tagebücher 1898–1916,* ed. Felix Klee. Cologne: 1957. Published as *Diaries: 1898–1918.* Berkeley: University of California, 1964.

———. 'Wege des Naturstudiums' (Paths of Nature Study), *Staatliches Bauhaus Weimar, 1919–23.* Munich, Weimar: 1923.

Lohmann-Siems, Isa. J. C. A. Grohmanns 'Ideen zu einer physiognomischen Anthropologie', aus den Jahren 1791. Eine Vorwegnahme kunsttheoretischer Gedanken des 20. Jahrhunderts (J. C. A. Grohmann's 'Ideas on a Physiognomical Anthropology', from 1791. An anticipation of the art theories of the twentieth century). *Yearbook of the Hamburg Art Collection,* Vol. 8, 1963.

———. Der universale Formbegriff in der Physiognomik des 18. Jahrhunderts. Ein Beitrag zur Geschichte der gegenwärtigen Kunsttheorie (The universal concept of form in physiognomics in the eighteenth century. Contribution to the history of present-day art theory). *Yearbook of the Hamburg Art Collection,* Vol. 9, 1964.

Pfeiffer-Belli, Erich. *Paul Klee.* Munich: 1964.

San Lazzaro, Gualtieri Di. *Paul Klee: Leben und Werk.* Munich, Zürich: 1958. Published as *Klee.* New York: Frederick A. Praeger, 1964.

Überwasser, Walter. 'Klees "Engel" und "Inseln"', *Festschrift Kurt Bauch* (Klee's Angels and Islands, Essays in Honour of Kurt Bauch). Berlin, Munich: 1957.

LAZLO MOHOLY-NAGY

Benjamin, Walter. *Das Kunstwerk im Zeitalter der technischen Reproduzierbarkeit* (Art in the Age of Technical Reproduction). Frankfurt: 1963.

Moholy-Nagy, Laszlo. 'Ismus oder Kunst' (Ism or Art), *Vis Voco,* Vol. V, No. 8/9, Leipzig, August–September, 1925.

———. *Malerei, Photographie, Film* (Painting, Photography, Film). Bauhaus Books, No. 8. Munich: 1925.

———. *The New Vision and Abstract of an Artist.* New York: George Wittenborn, 1947.

———. *60 Photos,* ed. Franz Roh. *Fototek,* Vol. 1, Berlin: 1930.

————. 'Zeitgemässe Typographie—Ziele, Praxis, Kritik' (Contemporary Typography—Its Aims, Practice, and Critique). *Offset, Buch und Werbekunst*, No. 7 (Bauhaus), Leipzig, 1926.

Moholy-Nagy, Sibyl. *Moholy-Nagy, A Biography*. New York: Harper & Row, 1950.

Wetter, Gustav A. *Sowjetideologie heute. Teil 1: Dialektischer und historischer Materialismus*. Fischer Books, Vol. 460. Frankfurt: 1962. Published as *Soviet Ideology Today*. New York: Frederick A. Praeger, 1966.

Catalogue

Lazlo Moholy-Nagy. Mannheim, Art Museum, July-August, 1961.

GEORG MUCHE

Muche, Georg. 'Bildende Kunst und Industrieform' (Fine arts and Art for Industry), *Bauhaus*, No. 1, 1926.

————. *Bilder, Fresken, Zeichnungen* (Paintings, Frescoes, Drawings). Introduction by Günther Wasmuth. Tübingen: 1954.

————. *Blickpunkt—Sturm, Dada, Bauhaus* (Vantage-Point—Sturm, Dada, Bauhaus). Munich: 1961.

————. *Das Versuchshaus des Bauhauses* (Experimental House at the Bauhaus, Weimar). Bauhaus Books, No. 3. Munich: 1925.

Richter, Horst, and Muche, Georg. *Monographien zur rheinisch-westfälischen Kunst der Gegenwart* (Monographs on present-day art in the Rhineland and Westphalia). Vol. 18. Recklinghausen: 1960.

Catalogue

Georg Muche: Gemälde—Zeichnungen—Graphik (Paintings, Drawings, Graphics). Exhibition in Munich, Municipal Gallery in the Lehnbachhaus, February–March, 1965.

OSKAR SCHLEMMER

Hildebrandt, Hans. *Oskar Schlemmer*. Includes a list of works and a bibliography. Munich: 1952.

Schlemmer, Oskar. *Abstraktion in Tanz und Kostüm* (Abstraction in Dance and Costume). 1928.

————. 'Analyse eines Bildes und andere Dinge' (Analysis of a Picture and Other Things). *Bauhaus*, Vol. III, No. 4, 1923.

————. *Briefe und Tagebücher* (Letters and Diaries), ed. Tut Schlemmer. Munich: 1958.

————. *Die Bühne am Bauhaus* (The Stage at the Bauhaus). Contributions by Schlemmer, Moholy-Nagy, and Farkas Monar. Bauhaus Books, No. 4. Munich: 1925. New edition, Mainz and Berlin: 1964.

Catalogue

Oskar Schlemmer 1888–1943. Exhibition at Berlin Academy of Arts, September–Oktober, 1963.

LOTHAR SCHREYER

Schreyer, Lothar. *Erinnerungen an Sturm und Bauhaus* (Memories of the Sturm and the Bauhaus). Munich: 1956.

—. *Kreuzigung* (Crucifixion). Dramatic work VIII, Competitive Stage Hamburg XX, Hamburg, 1920.

LIST OF PLATES

1. Lyonel Feininger
Kirche in Niedergrundstedt (Church at Niedergrundstedt) · **1919**
Oil on canvas, $39\frac{7}{8}$ x 49 in. (101 x 125 cm.), signed bottom left.
Galerie des 20. Jahrhunderts, Berlin
Hess 199

2. Lyonel Feininger
Mellingen V · 1917
India ink and water-colour, 8 x $9\frac{3}{4}$ in. (20.3 x 24.7 cm.), signed, titled, and dated in bottom margin.

3. Lyonel Feininger
Eichelborn · 1920
Oil on canvas, $31\frac{1}{2}$ x $38\frac{3}{4}$ in. (80 x 98.4 cm.), signed top right.
Bequest Preussischer Kulturbesitz, State Museums, National Gallery, Berlin
Private collection
Hess 208

4. Lyonel Feininger
Ober-Weimar VII (Upper Weimar VII) · **1920**
India ink and water-colour, $9\frac{1}{2}$ x $12\frac{1}{4}$ in. (23.5 x 31 cm.), signed, titled, and dated in bottom margin.
Stuttgart Art Gallery
Robert Norman Ketterer

5. Lyonel Feininger
Kleine Maske (Small Mask) · **1926**
Oil on canvas, $18\frac{7}{8}$ x $15\frac{3}{4}$ in. (48 x 40 cm.), signed bottom left.
Lyonel Feininger estate, New York
Hess 269

6. Lyonel Feininger
Barfüsserkirche in Erfurt I (Pilgrimage Church in Erfurt I) · **1924**
Oil on canvas, $47\frac{3}{8}$ x $43\frac{3}{4}$ in. (119 x 110 cm.), signed top right.
State Gallery, Stuttgart
Hess 248

7. Lyonel Feininger
Platz an der Kirche (Church Square) · **1921**
India ink and water-colour, 12 x $9\frac{1}{4}$ in. (30.5 x 23.5 cm.), signed, titled, and dated at bottom edge.
Private collection

8. Lyonel Feininger
Der Grützturm in Treptow (The Tower in Treptow) · **1928**
Oil on canvas, 40 x 32 in. (101.3 x 81 cm.), signed and dated top right.
Hessian State Museum, Darmstadt.
Hess 302

9. Lyonel Feininger
Gelbes Haus und kleine Figuren (Yellow House and Small Figures) · **1921**
India ink and water-colour, $9\frac{7}{8}$ x $11\frac{1}{4}$ in. (25 x 28.5 cm.), signed and dated in bottom margin.
Private collection

10. Lyonel Feininger
Blaue Marine (Blue Marine) · **1924**
Oil on canvas, $18\frac{3}{4}$ x $32\frac{3}{4}$ in. (47.5 x 83 cm.), signed and dated bottom right.
Munson Williams Proctor Institute, Utica, N.Y.
Hess 242

11. Lyonel Feininger
Gelmeroda IX · 1926
Oil on canvas, $39\frac{3}{8}$ x $31\frac{1}{2}$ in. (100 x 80 cm.), signed and dated top left.
Folkwang Museum, Essen
Hess 263

12. Lyonel Feininger
Marine (Hafen von Peppermint) (Marine—Peppermint Harbour) · **1929**
Oil on canvas, $11\frac{1}{4}$ x $16\frac{1}{2}$ in. (28.5 x 42 cm.), signed bottom right.
Private collection, Berne
Hess 319

13. Lyonel Feininger
Ankunft der Motorsegler (Arrival of the Motor Yachts) · **1930**
India ink and water-colour, $9\frac{1}{4}$ x $16\frac{1}{8}$ in. (23.5 x 41 cm.), signed, titled, and dated in bottom margin.
Private collection

14. Lyonel Feininger
Domchor, Halle (Cathedral Chancel, Halle) · **1931**
Oil on canvas, $39\frac{3}{8}$ x $32\frac{1}{4}$ in. (100 x 82 cm.), signed and dated top right.
Art Museum, Hamburg
Hess 335

15a. Lyonel Feininger
Das hohe Ufer (The Bay) · **1923**
Oil on canvas, $20\frac{1}{2}$ x $30\frac{1}{2}$ in. (52 x 77.5 cm.), signed and dated bottom right.
Private collection, Düsseldorf
Hess 234

15b. Lyonel Feininger
Dalmatien (Dalmatia) · **1934**
Oil on canvas, $15\frac{3}{4}$ x $18\frac{7}{8}$ in. (40 x 48 cm.), signed and dated top right.
Private collection, New York
Hess 365

16. Lyonel Feininger
Die blaue Insel (The Blue Island) · **1934**
Oil on canvas, $15\frac{3}{4}$ x $17\frac{7}{8}$ in. (40 x 48 cm.), signed top left.
Lyonel Feininger estate, New York
Hess 362

17. Lyonel Feininger
Das gestrandete Schiff (B e a c h e d V e s -
s e l) · **1922**
India ink and water-colour, 9¼ x 12¾ in.
(24 x 33 cm.), signed, titled, and dated in bottom margin.
Private collection

18. Johannes Itten
Der rote Turm (T h e R e d T o w e r) · **1918**
Oil on canvas, 55⅛ x 39⅜ in. (140 x 100 cm.),
signed and dated on reverse.
Private collection

19. Johannes Itten
Kinderbildnis (P o r t r a i t o f a C h i l d) ·
1922
Oil on panel, 43¼ x 35½ in. (110 x 90 cm.),
titled on scroll 'Johann Matthias Itten', dated
on the card in the child's hand, and signed
on reverse.
Private collection

20. Georg Muche
Komposition Graublau-Rosa (G r e y - B l u e
P i n k C o m p o s i t i o n) · **1921**
Oil on canvas, 28¼ x 18½ in. (72 x 47 cm.),
signed bottom right.
Muche collection, Lindau on Bodensee

21. Georg Muche
Zwei Eimer (T w o B u c k e t s) · **1923**
Oil on canvas, 39⅜ x 27¼ in. (100 x 69 cm.),
signed and dated bottom right.
Bauhaus Archive, Darmstadt

22. Georg Muche
Vier Akzente (F o u r A c c e n t s) · **1920**
Oil on canvas, 23⅝ x 18¼ in. (60 x 46 cm.),
signed on reverse.
Private collection

23. Georg Muche
Komposition mit schwarzer und grüner Form
(C o m p o s i t i o n w i t h B l a c k a n d
G r e e n F o r m s) · **1920**
Oil on canvas, 28 x 21¼ in. (71 x 54 cm.),
signed bottom right.
Municipal Art Collection, Bonn

24. Georg Muche
Verblühende Pflanzen (W i t h e r i n g
P l a n t s) · **1922**
Oil on canvas.
Whereabouts unknown

25. Lothar Schreyer
Mann (M a n)
Figure for full-length mask in the drama **Man.**
Water-colour and India ink on grey paper,
14⅝ x 12¼ in. (37 x 31 cm.), signed and dated
bottom right.
Schreyer collection, Hamburg

26a. Lothar Schreyer
**Totenbild des Mannes für das Totenhaus des
Mannes** (D e a t h P i c t u r e o f M a n f o r
t h e D e a t h H o u s e o f M a n) · **1920**
Painted wood. (See Schreyer, **Erinnerungen
an Sturm und Bauhaus,** pp. 158 ff.)

26b. Lothar Schreyer
**Maria im Mond; ihr zu Füssen der Tänzer
mit dem Tanzschild** (V i r g i n i n t h e
M o o n ; a t h e r F e e t t h e D a n c e r
w i t h t h e D a n c e S h i e l d)
Masks for the figures in **Mondspiel,** performed
at the Weimar Bauhaus in 1923

27. Oskar Schlemmer
Drei Profile (T h r e e P r o f i l e s) · **1922**
Tempera on paper, 17⅛ x 11¼ in. (43.5 x
28.5 cm.).
Private collection, Stuttgart
Hildebrandt 95

28. Oskar Schlemmer
Konzentrische Gruppe (C o n c e n t r i c
G r o u p) · **1925**
Oil on canvas, 38¼ x 24½ in. (97 x 62 cm.).
Württemberg State Gallery, Stuttgart
Hildebrandt 115

29. Oskar Schlemmer
Tischgesellschaft (C o m p a n y a t T a b l e) ·
1923
Oil on canvas, 28⅜ x 24⅝ in. (72 x 60 cm.).
Ida Bienert collection, Munich
Hildebrandt 103

30. Oskar Schlemmer
Abstrakte Figur—Rundplastik (A b s t r a c t
F i g u r e — S c u l p t u r e i n t h e r o u n d) ·
1921
Nickeled bronze, h. 42⅛ in. (107 cm.).

31. Oskar Schlemmer
Tänzerin—Die Geste (D a n c e r — T h e
G e s t u r e) · **1922/23**
Oil and tempera on canvas, 78¾ x 51⅛ in.
(200 x 130 cm.).
Tut Schlemmer collection, Stuttgart
Hildebrandt 97

32. Oskar Schlemmer
Vorübergehender (M a n P a s s i n g B y) ·
1924
Oil on canvas, 38¼ x 31½ in. (97 x 80 cm.).
Last in the collection of the Municipal Gallery,
Dresden; present whereabouts unknown
Hildebrandt 106

33. Oskar Schlemmer
Römisches (R o m a n) · **1925**
Oil on canvas, 38⅜ x 24⅜ in. (97.5 x 62 cm.).
Public Art Collection, Basle
Hildebrandt 110

34. Oskar Schlemmer
Zwischen Säulen (B e t w e e n C o l u m n s) ·
1928
Water-colour, 21⅝ x 17 in. (55 x 43 cm.).
Tut Schlemmer collection, Stuttgart
Hildebrandt 598

35. Oskar Schlemmer
Helle Vielfigurengruppe (G r o u p o f L i g h t -
c o l o u r e d F i g u r e s) · **1936**
Pencil and chalk, 26 x 19¾ in. (65.5 x 50 cm.).
Private collection

36. Oskar Schlemmer
Bauhaustreppe (Staircase at the Bauhaus) · **1932**
Water-colour, 10⅞ x 8⅝ in. (27.7 x 21.9 cm.).
Private collection, Darmstadt
Hildebrandt 744

37. Paul Klee
Häuser am Meer (Houses by the Sea) · **1920/134**
Water-colour, 9½ x 12½ in. (24 x 32 cm.), signed in the picture, right-hand side, titled and dated on bottom margin.
Private collection

38. Paul Klee
Gartenarchitektur (Garden Architecture) · **1919/158**
Oil on board, 17 x 15 in. (43 x 38 cm.), signed and dated bottom left.
Private collection

39. Paul Klee
Villa R. · **1919/153**
Tempera and oil, 10½ x 8¾ in. (26.5 x 22 cm.).
Public Art Collection, Basle
Grohmann 119

40. Paul Klee
Gespenst eines Genies (Spectre of a Genius) · **1922/10**
Water-colour, 20½ x 13¾ in. (52 x 35 cm.), signed top right, titled and dated on the border.
Private collection

41. Paul Klee
Rot-Violett-Gelbgrün Gestuft (Red/Violet/Yellow-Green, Terraced) · **1922/64**
Water-colour, 9¼ x 12¼ in. (23.5 x 31 cm.), signed in picture, right-hand side, titled and dated on the border.
Private collection

42. Paul Klee
Silbermondgeläute (Silver Moon Chimes) · **1923**
Water-colour, 10⅝ x 15 in. (27 x 38 cm.), signed bottom centre.
Private collection

43. Paul Klee
Stilleben mit dem Würfel (Still-life with the Die) · **1923/22**
Water-colour, 10⅝ x 15 in. (27 x 38 cm.), signed top centre, titled and dated on the border.
Private collection

44. Paul Klee
Mondspiel (Moon Game) · **1923/153**
Water-colour, 20 x 15½ in. (50.8 x 39.4 cm.), signed bottom right, dated and titled on the mount.
Bequest Preussischer Kulturbesitz, State Museums, National Gallery, Berlin

45. Paul Klee
Schauspieler (Actor) · **1923/27**
Oil on paper, 19⅞ x 10½ in. (50.5 x 26.5 cm.), signed top right, titled and dated on the border.
Private collection, Berne
Grohmann 179

46. Paul Klee
Bildnis vergangener Schönheit (Portrait of Faded Beauty) · **1924/11**
Oil on canvas, 17⅛ x 14⅜ in. (43.5 x 36.5 cm.), signed bottom left, titled and dated on the mount.
Private collection

47. Paul Klee
Dünenlandschaft Baltrum (Dunes at Baltrum) · **1923/119**
Water-colour, 9⅝ x 12⅜ in. (24.5 x 31.5 cm.), signed bottom right, titled and dated on the mount.
Private collection

48. Paul Klee
Fische—Aquarium (Fishes—Aquarium) · **1927/8**
Oil on gesso, 14 x 19½ in. (35.5 x 49.5 cm.), signed and dated bottom right.
Private collection

49. Paul Klee
Flora auf Sand (Flora on the Sand) · **1927/W6**
Water-colour, 9½ x 12 in. (23.5 x 30.5 cm.), signed bottom left, titled and dated on the mount.

50. Paul Klee
Sonnenuntergang (Sunset) · **1930/E9**
Oil on canvas, 18½ x 27½ in. (47 x 70 cm.), signed bottom left, titled and dated on the mount.
Private collection, Berlin
Grohmann 302

51. Paul Klee
Relativ Wägbares (Relative Weights) · **1930/3**
Water-colour, 13¼ x 12¼ in. (33.5 x 31 cm.), signed top right, titled and dated on the mount.
Private collection

52. Paul Klee
Letzter Schnee (Last Snow) · **1927/L9**
Oil on canvas, 12½ x 16½ in. (32 x 42 cm.), signed and dated top left, signed, dated, and titled on reverse.
Private collection

53. Paul Klee
Geist bei Wein und Spiel (Ghost with Glass and Dice) · **1927/K6**
Oil on canvas, 33½ x 26 in. (85 x 60 cm.), signed and dated bottom left.
Private collection

54. Paul Klee
Ein Fetzen Gemeinschaft (A Shred of Community) · **1932/X2**
Water-colour, 7 x 14 in. (18 x 36 cm.).
Private collection

55. Paul Klee
Grenze einer Wanderung (Limit of a Walk) · **1933/H8**
Water-colour, 8¼ x 12¾ in. (21 x 32.5 cm.), signed top left, titled and dated on the mount.
Private collection

56. Wassily Kandinsky
Schwarzer Raster (Black Grid) · **1922**
Oil on canvas, 37¾ x 41¾ in. (96 x 106 cm.), initialled and dated bottom left.
Private collection, Paris

57. Wassily Kandinsky
Komposition (Composition) · **1923**
India ink and water-colour, 15¾ x 16⅝ in. (40 x 42 cm.).
Private collection, Darmstadt

58. Wassily Kandinsky
Bogen und Spitze (Bow and Point) · **1923**
Oil, 18½ x 16⅝ in. (47 x 42 cm.), initialled and dated bottom left.
Museum of Non-Objective Art, New York

59. Wassily Kandinsky
Auf Weiss (On White) · **1923**
Oil on canvas, 41¼ x 38½ in. (105 x 98 cm.), initialled and dated bottom left.
Private collection, Paris
Grohmann 253

60. Wassily Kandinsky
Durchgehender Strich (Dividing Line) · **1923**
Oil on canvas, 45¼ x 78¾ in. (115 x 200 cm.), initialled and dated bottom left.
Nina Kandinsky, Paris, on loan to Basle Art Museum
Grohmann 255

61. Wassily Kandinsky
Gute Laune (Happy Mood) · **1923**
Water-colour, 10½ x 14¼ in. (27 x 36 cm.), initialled and dated bottom left.
Water-colour Catalogue No. 47
Private collection

62. Wassily Kandinsky
Spannung nach oben (Upward Tension) · **1924**
Water-colour, 19¼ x 13⅜ in. (49 x 34 cm.), initialled and dated bottom left.
Water-colour Catalogue No. 168
Private collection

63. Wassily Kandinsky
Scharfe Härte (Sharp Hardness) · **1926**
Oil on board, 24 x 13¾ in. (61 x 35 cm.), initialled and dated bottom left.
Private collection, Cologne
Grohmann 341

64. Wassily Kandinsky
Dicht umgeben (Closely Surrounded) · **1926**
Oil on canvas, 39⅜ x 25¼ in. (100 x 64 cm.), initialled and dated bottom left.
Private collection, Paris
Grohmann 370

65. Wassily Kandinsky
Oberes Zentrum (Upper Centre) · **1926**
Water-colour, 14⅜ x 10 in. (36.5 x 25.5 cm.), initialled and dated bottom left.
Water-colour Catalogue No. 208
Private collection

66. Wassily Kandinsky
Winklig (Angular) · **1927**
Oil on canvas, 22½ x 20½ in. (57 x 52 cm.), initialled and dated bottom left.
Private collection, Paris
Grohmann 386

67. Wassily Kandinsky
Quer und Hoch (Across and Up) · **1927**
Water-colour, 13¾ x 17⅞ in. (35 x 45.5 cm.), initialled and dated bottom left.
Water-colour Catalogue No. 215
Private collection

68. Wassily Kandinsky
Verschleiertes Glühen (Veiled Glow) · **1928**
Oil on board, 30¼ x 24½ in. (77 x 62 cm.), initialled and dated bottom left.
Private collection, New York
Grohmann 422

69. Wassily Kandinsky
Schwarz-Rot (Black-Red) · **1927**
Oil on canvas, 17¾ x 26 in. (45 x 66 cm.), initialled and dated bottom left.
Private collection, Paris
Grohmann 405

70. Wassily Kandinsky
Zwischen Hell (Between the Light) · **1931**
Oil on board, 27½ x 31½ in. (70 x 80 cm.), initialled and dated bottom left.
Private collection, Brussels
Grohmann 559

71. Wassily Kandinsky
In Einander (Intermingling) · **1928**
Water-colour, 18⅞ x 8⅝ in. (28 x 22 cm.), initialled and dated bottom left.
Water-colour Catalogue No. 248
Private collection

72. Wassily Kandinsky
Mitte Blau (Centre Blue) · **1928**
Water-colour, 19⅛ x 12½ in. (48.5 x 32 cm.), initialled and dated bottom left.
Water-colour Catalogue No. 254
Private collection

73. Wassily Kandinsky
Kreis und Fleck (C i r c l e a n d S p o t) ·
1929
Oil on canvas, 30 x 26 in. (76 x 66 cm.), initialled
and dated bottom left.
Private collection, Paris
Grohmann 442

74. Wassily Kandinsky
Dreizehn Rechtecke (T h i r t e e n R e c-
t a n g l e s) · **1930**
Oil on board, 27½ x 23½ in. (70 x 60 cm.),
initialled and dated bottom left.
Private collection, Paris
Grohmann 525

75. Wassily Kandinsky
Sanfter Nachdruck (G e n t l e E m p h a s i s) ·
1931
Oil on panel, 39⅜ x 39⅜ in. (100 x 100 cm.),
initialled and dated bottom left.
Private collection, New York
Grohmann 549

76. Wassily Kandinsky
Ausgleich-Rosa (P i n k E q u i l i b r i u m) ·
1933
Oil and tempera on canvas, 36¼ x 28¾ in.
(92 x 73 cm.), initialled and dated bottom left.
Private collection, Paris
Grohmann 583

77. Laszlo Moholy-Nagy
4 (1920): Die grosse Gefühlsmaschine (T h e
G r e a t E m o t i o n M a c h i n e) · **1920**
Oil on canvas, 37⅝ x 29½ in. (95.5 x 75 cm.),
signed bottom right.
Private collection, Munich

78. Laszlo Moholy-Nagy
Das grosse Eisenbahnbild (T h e L a r g e
R a i l w a y P i c t u r e) · **1920**
Oil on canvas, 39⅜ x 30¾ in. (100 x 78 cm.),
signed bottom right.
Private collection

79. Laszlo Moholy-Nagy
KL 8 · **1922**
Collage on red paper, 26½ x 19¾ in. (75 x
49 cm.), signed bottom left.
Private collection

80. Laszlo Moholy-Nagy
A XX · **1924**
Oil on canvas, 54 x 46 in. (136 x 115.5 cm.).
Klihm Art Gallery, Munich

81. Laszlo Moholy-Nagy
Q IV · **1923**
Oil on canvas, 29⅞ x 37⅝ in. (76 x 95.5 cm.),
signed and dated on reverse.
Private collection, Munich

82. Laszlo Moholy-Nagy
Z VIII · **1924**
Oil on canvas, 44⅞ x 52 in. (114 x 132 cm.),
signed, titled, and dated on reverse.
Bequest Preussischer Kulturbesitz, State Mu-
seums, National Gallery, Berlin

83. Laszlo Moholy-Nagy
Z III · **1922**
Oil on canvas, 37¾ x 29¾ in. (96 x 75.5 cm.),
signed on reverse.
Private collection

84. Herbert Bayer
Wolkenbild (C l o u d s c a p e) · **1928**
Gouache, 10⅝ x 17 in. (27 x 43 cm.), signed
bottom right.
Klihm Art Gallery, Munich

85. Herbert Bayer
Holz im Wald (T i m b e r i n t h e F o r e s t) ·
1930/13
Water-colour, 13½ x 18¾ in. (34.2 x 47.5 cm.),
signed and dated bottom right.
Klihm Art Gallery, Munich

86. Herbert Bayer
Abstraktion, blau—Komposition im Raum
(A b s t r a c t i o n, B l u e — C o m p o s i-
t i o n i n S p a c e) · **1928/11**
Water-colour and gouache, 11⅞ x 18½ in.
(30 x 47 cm.), signed and dated bottom right.
Klihm Art Gallery, Munich

87. Herbert Bayer
Wolken und Rahmen (C l o u d s a n d
F r a m e s) · **1928/11**
Gouache, 10⅝ x 17 in. (17 x 43 cm.), signed
and dated bottom right.
Klihm Art Gallery, Munich

88. Josef Albers
Hochbauten (T a l l B u i l d i n g s) · **1927**
Fused glass, white in black (opaque), sand-
blown, 13 x 13 in. (33 x 33 cm.).
Private collection, Dallas, Texas

89. Josef Albers
Glasfenster (G l a s s W i n d o w)
Stained glass and bottle fragments set in
brass, 20½ x 15⅜ in. (52 x 39 cm.).
Albers collection, New Haven, Conn.

90. Josef Albers
Gebündelt (B u n d l e d) · **1925**
Fused glass (transparent), dull ground, sand-
blown, black. Painted and baked on pink gold.
Reverse etched, frosted. 12½ x 13 in. (31.8 x
33 cm.).
Albers collection, New Haven, Conn.

91. Josef Albers
Falsch gewickelt II (F a l s e C o i l I I) ·
1931
Fused glass, white in black (opaque), sand-
blown, black frosted with grey, 19½ x 19¾ in.
(49.5 x 49.8 cm.).

On Dust Jacket:
Josef Albers
Wandschirme (F o l d i n g S c r e e n s) · **1928**
Red fused glass (opaque), with sand-blown
white, and painted and fired black. 13⅞ x
17½ in. (35 x 44.5 cm.).
Private collection, Dallas, Texas.